The Stoicism Bible

Cultivating Inner Strength and Resilience Embracing Stoic Wisdom for a Life of Purpose, Fulfillment, and Lasting Impact

LUCIUS KNOWLES

TABLE OF CONTENTS

INTRODUCTION 1
Understanding Stoicism in Modern Life 2

Part 1: The Essence Of Stoicism

1. WHAT IS STOICISM? 9
Historical Origins 9
Core Stoic Principles 12

2. THE STOIC PHILOSOPHERS 14
Profiles of Key Stoic Thinkers 14
Their Contributions to Stoicism 16

Part 2: Daily Stoic Practices

3. FINDING INNER PEACE 21
Techniques for Managing Stress and Anxiety 23
Stoic Meditation 25

4. BUILDING RESILIENCE 28
Developing Emotional Strength 28
External Circumstances vs. Internal Perceptions 29
Mindfulness & Self-Awareness 29
Actively Strengthening Emotional Resilience 29
Techniques to Develop Emotional Strength 30
Cultivating Emotional Strength in Everyday Life 30
The Path Towards Unshakable Resilience 31
Handling Adversity with Stoic Wisdom 31
The Gift of Perspective 31
Universal Interconnectedness 32
Control vs. Influence 32
The Art of Practicing Misfortune 33
Compassion as a Remedy for Adversity 33

5. CULTIVATING VIRTUE 34
The Stoic Virtues: Wisdom, Courage, Justice, Temperance 34
The Communion of Virtues 36
Practicing Virtue in Daily Life 36

Part 3: Stoicism In Relationships

6. STOIC RELATIONSHIPS 41
Applying Stoicism to Friendships and Family 43
Resolving Conflicts Stoically 45

7. STOIC PARENTING 47
Raising Virtuous Children with Stoic Values 50
Instilling Stoic Resilience in Kids 52

Part 4: Stoicism In The Modern World

8. STOICISM IN THE WORKPLACE 59
Becoming a Stoic Leader 61
Stoic Problem-Solving at Work 63

9. STOICISM AND SOCIAL IMPACT 66
Stoic Ethics and Social Responsibility 68
Advocating for Positive Change 70

Part 5: Advanced Stoicism

10. STOIC ETHICS 75
The Stoic Code of Conduct 77
Living a Stoic Life 79

11. STOIC HAPPINESS 83
The Stoic Definition of Happiness 83
Pursuing Eudaimonia 85

Part 6: Mastering Stoicism

12. STOIC CHALLENGES AND OBSTACLES 91
Overcoming Common Hurdles 93
Dealing with Stoic Criticism 95

13. THE STOIC LIFESTYLE 98
Practical Tips for Embracing Stoicism Daily 98
Creating Your Stoic Routine 100

Part 7: The Future Of Stoicism

14. STOICISM IN THE DIGITAL AGE 105
Applying Stoicism in a Technology-Driven World 105
Stoic Mindfulness in the Digital Era 107

15. INSPIRING FUTURE GENERATIONS 109
Teaching Stoicism to the Next Generation 109
Stoicism in Education 111

CONCLUSION: THE EVERLASTING WISDOM OF STOICISM 114

Introduction

In the pursuit of a meaningful and resilient life, countless individuals have turned to the ancient wisdom of Stoicism. The *"Stoicism Bible"* serves as an essential companion for those seeking to explore and embrace this transformative philosophy rooted in practical action and profound insights. Whether you are a long-time adherent or simply curious about its principles, this comprehensive guide presents the pillars of Stoicism and their relevance in today's fast-paced world.

The book begins by chronicling the rich history of Stoicism, introducing readers to its founding figures such as Seneca, Epictetus, and Marcus Aurelius. Through their thoughts and experiences, we witness how Stoic principles guided these influential leaders towards virtue, wisdom, and inner peace in times of both turmoil and prosperity.

As we delve deeper into the core tenets of Stoicism, the *"Stoicism Bible"* highlights essential teachings on rationality, self-discipline, emotional control, resilience against suffering, and the indomitable human spirit. By vividly illustrating key concepts with real-life examples and inspiring stories from history's most remarkable Stoics, this book empowers readers to harness these lessons in their own lives.

Equally crucial to understanding Stoic philosophy is recognizing its limitations and common misconceptions. This book provides an honest appraisal of its criticisms while offering counterarguments that demonstrate its enduring relevance in our modern lives.

To facilitate practical application, the "*Stoicism Bible*" equips readers with essential exercises designed to instill Stoic principles into their daily routines. From reflecting on one's own character to developing mindful habits in adversity, these actionable practices foster personal growth and self-improvement.

The journey towards a more fulfilling life begins with self-discovery - a process that is aided by timeless wisdom shared across generations. The "*Stoicism Bible*" brings together these invaluable teachings to help seekers embark on a path towards inner strength and serenity. Embark on this transformative learning experience, and uncover the lasting power of Stoicism.

Understanding Stoicism in Modern Life

Stoicism, an ancient philosophy rooted in Greek and Roman times, may seem like a distant concept to our modern, fast-paced world. However, upon closer examination, we quickly realize that the core principles of Stoicism remain highly relevant today. In essence, Stoicism is a practical philosophy that teaches us how to live a content and fulfilled life by focusing on elements within our control and accepting those beyond it.

In this rapidly changing world where stress and anxiety often dominate our lives, understanding and applying Stoic principles can act as a guiding beacon. With an emphasis on personal growth and self-improvement, Stoicism encourages us to face our fears, manage emotions, and seek tranquility while understanding the impermanence of life.

The central tenet of Stoicism is the understanding that true happiness can only be achieved when we focus on aspects of our lives that we can control. These include our thoughts, beliefs, emotions, actions, and reactions. By doing so, we minimize the impact of external factors such as other peoples' opinions or uncontrollable events.

Epictetus, a renowned Stoic philosopher, once said: "We cannot choose our external circumstances but we can always choose how we respond to them." This perspective implies that although we cannot control everything around us (politics, other people's behaviors or opinions), we possess the power to regulate our interpretations and emotional reactions to these circumstances.

Another essential aspect of Stoicism is the practice of mindfulness. The philosophy emphasizes being present in each moment without judgment or attachment. It teaches individuals to appreciate what they have rather than yearn for more – advocating for gratitude over greed.

Through mindfulness practices such as meditation and journaling, Stoics develop greater self-awareness and the ability to disengage from negative thought patterns or harmful emotions. By becoming truly aware of one's thoughts and feelings without succumbing to them, it becomes easier to maintain a sense of tranquility even amongst the chaos of modern life.

Memento Mori, a Stoic principle, roughly translates to "remember that you will die." While this may sound morbid, it serves as a powerful reminder that life is short and precious. Stoics perceive this principle not as a doomsday prophecy, but rather as motivation to be diligent with our time, focus on meaningful pursuits, and cherish the present moment. This concept can help us to release ourselves from the anxieties and stressors of everyday existence by putting them into perspective.

The Dichotomy of Control, another Stoic concept, is essentially the understanding that some things are within our control while others aren't. In modern times, we're bombarded with information that often causes us to worry about events occurring across the globe – events which we have no power over. Stoicism teaches us to differentiate between our areas of influence and things outside it. By doing so, we become more resilient in the face of setbacks and less reactive to events beyond our control.

Moreover, Stoicism discusses the importance of personal virtues such as wisdom, courage, justice, and temperance. While these virtues might not be explicitly discussed in modern society, they remain as crucial now as they were thousands of years ago. By cultivating these qualities in ourselves, we become better citizens and leaders – contributing pos communities.

Resilience is a significant theme within Stoic philosophy which resonates strongly with contemporary living. Stoicism provides valuable strategies for individuals seeking to bounce back from setbacks or adversity – whether those entails losing a job or experiencing a challenging personal situation. By practicing stoic methods like visualization or finding silver linings in difficult circumstances, individuals can become more adaptable and prepared for life's inevitable hurdles.

Applying stoic principles in modern life involves embracing a few key tenets:

1. Embrace rationality: Rationality is at the heart of Stoicism. Rational thinking allows us to reflect on our beliefs and question their origins. By doing so, we learn to differentiate between what we have control over (our beliefs) and what we do not (other people's actions). This creates a sense of stability in our lives that empowers us to engage with obstacles head-on instead of avoiding them due to fear.

2. Practice virtue: Virtue is another primary concept in Stoicism. When faced with choices or actions in our daily lives, we should seek to act according to the four cardinal virtues – wisdom, courage, justice, and temperance. By focusing on these virtues in every decision we make, we contribute positively to both ourselves and society as a whole.

3. Accept fate: One of the core concepts in Stoicism is Fatalism or accepting whatever comes into your life without resistance. While this may seem counterintuitive initially, the idea is to embrace the present moment and any challenges it may bring rather than constantly pushing against it. This acceptance is meant to foster inner resilience and peace, as well as reduce negative emotions like worry or anxiety.

4. View situations objectively: In modern life, we often encounter situations that elicit strong emotional responses from us. The Stoic practice of viewing situations objectively can help mitigate these extreme emotions by encouraging us to recognize, analyze, and understand our feelings instead of being blindly guided by them. This approach promotes level-headedness and helps us make decisions based on reason rather than emotion.

5. Understand the impermanence of things: Stoicism teaches that everything in life is temporary and subject to change. By recognizing the impermanent nature of all things, we learn to detach from material possessions and the pursuit of superficial happiness. Instead, we become more focused on developing a strong inner character that is not reliant on external circumstances for contentment.

6. Practice gratitude: As part of embracing Stoicism in modern life, it is essential to cultivate an attitude of gratitude. Gratitude allows us to appreciate what we have, no matter how little, instead of constantly trying to chase after more or feeling unsatisfied with our current situation. This shift in perspective can significantly improve our overall well-being and happiness.

7. Engage in self-reflection: Another key aspect of Stoicism is the practice of self-reflection and introspection. By examining our thoughts, beliefs, and actions regularly, we gain a deeper understanding of ourselves and what motivates us. This self-awareness allows us to make better choices aligned with our values and contributes to personal growth.

8. Foster resilience: Lastly, adopting a Stoic mindset can lead to increased resilience in the face of adversity. By understanding that hardships are bound to happen in life – regardless of planning or effort – we become more equipped to deal with difficulties when they arise without becoming overwhelmed or discouraged.

Part 1: The Essence Of Stoicism

In Part 1, we delve into the essence of Stoicism, exploring its historical origins and core principles that have captivated minds for centuries. You'll learn about key Stoic thinkers, their contributions to this timeless philosophy, and how their wisdom can serve as a foundation for your pursuit of a meaningful and purpose-driven life.

Chapter 1

What is Stoicism?

Historical Origins

In the annals of philosophical thought, Stoicism holds a prominent position as a school that has withstood the test of time and continues to influence contemporary life. Its origins can be traced back to ancient Greece, where it was developed in response to the turbulence and unpredictability of life. The foundations of Stoicism were laid by a diverse array of minds, whose collective understanding helped create the principles and strategies that have inspired countless individuals through millennia.

The earliest roots of Stoicism can be found in Athens, in the late 4th century BCE. At that time, an unassuming merchant named Zeno of Citium found himself shipwrecked, stranded in the bustling metropolis. Zeno began attending lectures by Crates the Cynic who introduced him to the tenets of Cynicism – a philosophy emphasizing virtue through austerity, shunning material wealth and societal expectations.

While Zeno admired Cynicism's principles, he felt it lacked practical applications for daily life. Thus, he ventured into his philosophical journey, drawing on the works of other notable philosophers such as Socrates and Heraclitus. In 301 BCE, Zeno established the Stoa Poikile (Painted Porch) in Athens – an open meeting place where people gathered to discuss ideas – and so began the Stoa philosophia or "philosophy of the Porch," which later evolved into Stoicism.

Zeno's teachings garnered considerable attention, marked by three central ideas: Logos (the rational structure governing reality), Physis (the natural world), and Ethos (human nature). He postulated that living in harmony with cosmic reason would lead to tranquility through inner fortitude and harmonious coexistence with fellow humans.

After Zeno's death in 262 BCE, one of his pupils Cleanthes assumed leadership at Stoa Poikile. Transmitted through fragments like "Hymn to Zeus," Cleanthes' works reveal a deep respect for Zeno's teachings, while also contributing his thoughts on the human psyche and physical world. As the second headmaster of the Stoa, Cleanthes bolstered Stoicism, expanding its influence throughout Athens and beyond.

Despite Cleanthes' efficacy, it was Chrysippus of Soli (280–207 BCE) – the third headmaster of Stoa Poikile – who consolidated the core tenets of Stoicism. Chrysippus delved into logic, ethics, and physics, penning numerous works (though very few have survived). He concluded that rationality governs the universe, also affirming that individuals possess free will through their reasoning abilities. As such, humans could control their responses to external events despite inevitable suffering. Essentially, Chrysippus fortified Stoic thought and paved its course for future philosophers.

While Stoicism had firmly taken root in Athens by this point, it would soon find a new home in Rome. Influential figures like Cato the Younger adopted its principles as a way to navigate chaotic political landscapes. It is in Rome that two of the most famous Stoic philosophers emerged: Epictetus and Seneca.

Epictetus (50–135 CE), a former slave turned philosopher, taught Stoicism with a central focus on personal accountability and embracing adversity as a tool for growth. He held no high regard for material possession or societal standing since neither dictated one's ability to live virtuously. Rather, he posited that genuine happiness derives from self-mastery and urged followers to challenge their perception of circumstances.

Around the same time as Epictetus lived Lucius Annaeus Seneca (4 BCE - 65 CE), born into a wealthy Roman family. As a playwright, statesman, and philosopher, Seneca navigated high society with equal parts intellect and tact. His writings advise on the practical applications of Stoic tenets amidst the distractions of affluence. Compassion, humility, and restraint are the pillars of Seneca's Stoicism, offering guidance for life's complexities.

Finally, we have Marcus Aurelius (121–180 CE), Roman emperor and philosopher king. The Meditations, his introspective journal, exemplifies Stoic principles in action. Aurelius grappled with the absolute power he possessed over the realm while questioning how to remain humble and just. He struggled to maintain his virtue amidst ceaseless external forces demanding his attention.

Throughout history, the Stoic philosophers encountered tribulations inherent to human existence – a tumultuous life, power struggles, and hardship. Despite these adversities, they forged a practical, timeless philosophy to help individuals cultivate inner peace. Stoicism's endurance can be attributed to its universality, applicable to anyone, anywhere, facing any form of life's challenges.

In the centuries that followed the Roman Empire, Stoicism continued to percolate through Western thought - informing the works of early Christian thinkers like Augustine of Hippo and later on Renaissance humanists such as Michel de Montaigne and Justus Lipsius. The 17th-century Dutch philosopher Baruch Spinoza also borrowed from Stoic ideas in his meditations on ethics and rationality.

Modern Stoicism further evolved with studies in cognitive behavioral therapy (CBT) drawing on its core belief that we have control over our perceptions and emotional responses. In times of great uncertainty and change, Stoicism provides a philosophical compass that has helped countless people navigate both personal challenges and societal upheavals with clarity and resilience.

It is with good reason that Stoicism has resonated across millennia: its timeless teachings encourage us to consistently evaluate our beliefs and behaviors in pursuit of virtuous living – a journey so many still embark upon today. Whether in ancient Athens or modern society, the essence of Stoicism remains a guiding light towards inner serenity and outside harmony.

Core Stoic Principles

Stoicism teaches us how to cultivate an inner sense of tranquility amidst external chaos, ultimately fostering wisdom, resilience, and peace of mind. The core principles outlined below are the foundation of the Stoic philosophy and serve as a guide to living a virtuous life.

1. Virtue is the Highest Good: At the heart of Stoic ethics is the belief that virtue is the ultimate good in life and the foundation for human flourishing. Virtue comes from our ability to reason and encompasses wisdom, courage, justice, and self-discipline. By practicing these virtues, we can develop our character and lead a fulfilling life.

2. Accept What You Cannot Control: Stoics believe that some things are within our control, while others are not. Differentiating between what we can and cannot control allows us to focus our energy on taking intentional actions in pursuit of virtue rather than becoming bogged down by external circumstances. One should accept whatever is outside one's control without longing for change or fearing loss.

3. Embrace Adversity as an Opportunity for Growth: The Stoics teach that adversity is an opportunity to exercise our virtues and develop our character. Instead of avoiding or resisting hardship, we should embrace it with open arms as a path for growth and self-improvement.

4. Cultivate Emotional Resilience: Emotional resilience refers to our ability to remain calm and focused even in challenging situations. This resilience comes from the recognition that it is not external events that cause emotional distress but rather our judgments about those events. By examining and reframing these judgments, we can maintain our equanimity in the face of adversity.

5. Practice Mindfulness: Mindfulness involves being fully present in each moment, aware of our thoughts, emotions, and sensations. In being mindful, the Stoics teach that we can gain a sense of clarity and control over our lives. Practicing mindfulness helps us pay closer attention to our thoughts, making it easier to identify cognitive distortions and negative judgments that may be contributing to emotional distress.

6. Live with Purpose and Meaning: Stoicism emphasizes living in accordance with nature and following our rational human instincts. By cultivating a life of purpose and aligning ourselves with our core values, we can find meaning in life and contribute positively to the world around us.

7. Focus on the Present: The Stoics believe that dwelling on the past or worrying about the future distracts us from living fully in the present moment. By focusing on the here and now, we can take meaningful actions that align with our values and make the most of each day.

8. Foster Gratitude: Gratitude plays a critical role in Stoic thought, as it helps cultivate a positive mindset by recognizing and appreciating the many good things we have in life. By regularly practicing gratitude, we can shift our focus from what we lack to what we have, promoting contentment.

9. Engage in Negative Visualization: Negative visualization involves imagining challenging scenarios or hardships as a way to develop resilience and mental fortitude. By contemplating potential negative outcomes, Stoics are better prepared to cope with these challenges should they arise while also fostering a greater appreciation for their current circumstances.

10. Develop Empathy Towards Others: Stoicism teaches that all people are united by their capacity for reason, thus fostering a sense of empathy towards others. This empathy allows us to better understand one another's experiences and motivations, ultimately promoting cooperation and community.

Incorporating these core principles into daily practice strengthens not only one's character but also one's ability to navigate life's challenges effectively. By embracing these tenets, practitioners gain perspective on their place in the world, cultivating virtues that foster wisdom, resilience, and inner peace.

Chapter 2

The Stoic Philosophers

Profiles of Key Stoic Thinkers

In this chapter, we will profile some of the most influential Stoic thinkers who contributed to its development and legacy.

1. Zeno of Citium (c. 334 – c. 262 BC): Zeno was a Hellenistic philosopher who founded the Stoic school of philosophy around 300 BC. Born in Citium, a city on the island of Cyprus, he was the son of a merchant. After losing his fortune in a shipwreck, he arrived in Athens and began studying under various philosophers such as Crates the Cynic and Polemo the Platonist.

Physically Zeno was often described as thin and somber, with a serious demeanor that contributed to his nickname "the Palestinian Pharaoh." He dressed simply, consistent with the Cynic tradition. Though he did not write extensive treatises like later philosophers, his teachings, recorded by his students and followers, emphasized living in harmony with nature and cultivating virtue through wisdom, self-discipline, and emotional resilience.

2. Cleanthes (c. 330 – c. 230 BC): Cleanthes was one of Zeno's most loyal disciples and succeeded him as the head of the Stoic school. Born in Assos (present-day Turkey), he came from a humble background and worked as a boxer before arriving in Athens to study philosophy.

Cleanthes is known for his ascetic lifestyle; he lived modestly even after attaining significant renown. Nicknamed "the Well," he believed in practicing what he preached—limiting personal possessions and eating simple meals.

Of all his writings attributed to him, only fragments survive today, such as his "Hymn to Zeus," where he praised the orderliness of the universe and its divine ruler.

3. Chrysippus (c. 280 – c. 207 BC): Following Cleanthes as the head of the Stoic school, Chrysippus was a prolific writer and a central figure in the development of Stoic philosophy. Born in Soli, near present-day Mersin, Turkey, he initially studied under the philosopher Cleanthes and later assumed leadership of the school.

Chrysippus displayed exceptional intelligence and an insatiable intellectual curiosity. He wrote more than 700 works on various subjects, ranging from ethics and logic to natural philosophy. Unfortunately, only fragments of his writing exist today.

His contemporaries viewed him as an impressive figure with a strong personality. Despite his intellectual prowess, he exhibited an eccentric lifestyle marked by bouts of heavy drinking and apparent indifference toward personal hygiene.

4. Epictetus (c. 50 – c. 135 AD): Born into slavery in Hierapolis, present-day Turkey, Epictetus later gained his freedom and became one of Rome's most prominent Stoic philosophers. His master allowed him to study philosophy under Musonius Rufus, another influential Stoic thinker of that time.

Epictetus was known for his practical approach to philosophy as a way of life. A crippled leg caused by mistreatment during his time as a slave did not hinder his ability to teach or write about Stoicism; instead, it likely fueled his interest in Stoic teachings on resilience and accepting one's circumstances. He authored "The Discourses" and "The Enchiridion," which remain essential texts for students of Stoicism today.

5. Marcus Aurelius (121 – 180 AD): Marcus Aurelius, Roman Emperor from 161 to 180 AD, is regarded as the last of the Five Good Emperors. Despite wielding immense political power that often leads to corruption, Marcus Aurelius remained steadfastly committed to Stoic principles throughout his life.

His Stoic education began under the tutelage of several private tutors, most notably Rusticus and Quintus Junius. He also studied independently, engaging with texts from the previous Stoic philosophers mentioned in this chapter.

His most significant contribution to the world is his personal journal known as "Meditations." Written during his military campaigns, it contains his reflections on life, virtue, and how he sought to apply Stoic principles to cope with the challenges and uncertainties of governance.

Their Contributions to Stoicism

This section will discuss the significant ideas and teachings of five key Stoic philosophers: Zeno of Citium, Cleanthes, Chrysippus, Epictetus, and Marcus Aurelius. Their collective works and ideas helped shape the school of thought into what we know today as Stoicism.

1. Zeno of Citium (c. 334 – c. 262 BC): Zeno of Citium, the founder of Stoicism, began his philosophical journey after he was shipwrecked on a voyage from his hometown in Cyprus. As a result, he found himself in Athens, where he studied under Crates, a Cynic philosopher. Influenced by Cynicism and Socratic tradition, he began lecturing at the Painted Stoa in Athens, marking the start of Stoicism.

Zeno contributed significantly to Stoic philosophy with his focus on ethics. His idea of the highest good was living according to reason or "logos," emphasizing self-control and indifference to external events or circumstances. According to Zeno, emotions stemmed from false judgments and led people away from virtue.

2. Cleanthes (c. 330 – c. 230 BC): As a student of Zeno's school and his successor as headmaster, Cleanthes expanded upon the foundations laid by his teacher. He is known for composing a hymn devoted to Zeus which elucidates his belief in divine providence and cosmic order. This hymn extols blissful adherence to Zeus's divine plan.

Cleanthes also added depth to Stoic philosophy by further segmenting Zeno's concept of virtue into three categories: rationality (the ability to make intelligent decisions), bravery (facing adversity without fear), and self-control (resisting desires that may lead one astray). Through these distinctions, Cleanthes emphasized the importance of internal virtues over material pursuits.

3. Chrysippus (c. 280 – c. 207 BC): Chrysippus built upon the work of his predecessors and is credited with solidifying Stoicism as a prominent school of thought during his time as headmaster. Often called the "Second Founder of Stoicism," Chrysippus was prolific in writing on a wide range of subjects, although much of his work has been lost over time.

He refined the Stoic idea that all emotions originate from inaccurate judgments and introduced new concepts to the philosophy, such as the "unity of virtues," which stated that individual virtues cannot truly exist without one another. This concept reflected in Chrysippus's belief that wisdom was ultimately the culmination of all virtues.

4. Epictetus (c. 50 – c. 135 AD): Epictetus, a former slave who became a renowned Stoic philosopher, focused on practical applications of Stoic teachings in everyday life. His works were recorded by his student Arrian in texts called Discourses and Handbook (Enchiridion).

Epictetus emphasized the dichotomy of control, urging individuals to focus on what is within their control (thoughts, beliefs, actions) and disregard external events beyond their influence. According to Epictetus, living an ethically good life meant maintaining rationality amid distressing situations and accepting whatever life brought with equanimity.

5. Marcus Aurelius (121 – 180 AD): Marcus Aurelius was not only a Roman emperor but also an ardent follower of Stoicism whose philosophical reflections can be found in his work Meditations. Written as a series of personal notes for self-improvement, Meditations is now regarded as one of the greatest contributions to Stoic literature.

Marcus Aurelius contemplated topics such as resilience, gratitude, duty, humility, and understanding the human condition. His reflections on the impermanence of life, personal responsibility, and reasoning embody core Stoic tenets. He encouraged the notion of daily self-examination to identify areas for self-improvement and emphasized moral virtues over external achievements.

Part 2: Daily Stoic Practices

In Part 2 of the Stoicism Bible, we focus on integrating Stoic principles into daily life through practical tools and techniques. Learn how to find inner peace by managing stress and anxiety using proven Stoic methods. Discover ways to build resilience through emotional strength, equipping you to handle adversity with a grounded perspective. Finally, engage in deep reflection on cultivating virtue as we examine the four cardinal virtues of Stoicism - wisdom, courage, justice, and temperance - and their role in our everyday lives.

Chapter 3

Finding Inner Peace

ACHIEVING INNER PEACE IS A CORNERSTONE OF THE STOIC philosophy. The goal of many ancient Stoics was to reach a state of tranquility, free from inner turmoil and the distractions of the outside world. In this pursuit, they focused on developing resilience against hardship and refining their character, which ultimately resulted in personal growth and self-mastery.

In a time where distractions are abundant and stressors are never far from us, it has never been more challenging to find inner peace. However, by embracing the teachings of the Stoic philosophers, we can cultivate an inner sanctuary that guards us against life's tumultuous nature.

To embark on your journey towards finding inner peace, consider incorporating these timeless Stoic practices into your daily routine:

1. Focus on what is within your control: The Stoics believed that focusing on what is within our control and letting go of that which lies beyond our influence can lead to a serenity unlike any other. Differentiating between the two can be difficult, but realizing this distinction is crucial in managing our emotional well-being.

Accepting the fact that some things lie outside of our control allows us to practice mindfulness and enjoy each moment without excessive anxiety.

While we may not have any direct influence over world events or the behavior of others, our thoughts and actions remain within our realm of control.

2. Cultivate self-awareness through reflection: Stoicism encourages regular self-assessment to help us identify areas for potential growth and reinforce positive habits. Taking time each day to reflect on your thoughts, emotions, and actions can improve your ability to respond effectively to various situations.

Introspection enables you to recognize patterns in your behavior and draw connections between how certain events or circumstances affect you mentally or emotionally. By identifying these patterns and actively working towards changing them, you can take charge of your life rather than succumbing to external influences.

3. Manage negative emotions through reframing: Stoics recognized the power of perspective in shaping our emotional well-being. Rather than allowing negative emotions to consume us, we can reframe situations that evoke such feelings. It is not the events themselves that cause us distress, but rather our judgment of them.

When faced with adversity, remind yourself that it is an opportunity for growth and spiritual development. When confronted with disappointment or frustration, acknowledge the situation for what it is—a temporary obstacle —and then focus on finding solutions rather than dwelling on misfortunes.

4. Practice gratitude: Gratitude was highly regarded by the Stoics as a means of promoting inner peace. Maintaining a grateful mindset enables us to recognize and appreciate the multitude of blessings that surround us daily.

By focusing on what you are grateful for—such as your health, loved ones, or opportunities for personal growth—you shift your attention away from negativity and cultivate feelings of contentment and inner harmony.

5. Embrace adversity as a means to growth: Stoicism teaches that adversity is an essential component in our quest for inner peace. Facing challenges head-on not only builds resilience but also strengthens our character and equips us to tackle future obstacles more effectively.

Instead of viewing setbacks as defeats, acknowledge them as critical tests designed to refine your resilience and self-discipline—an opportunity to put your Stoic principles into action.

6. Practice self-discipline: Discipline was an essential virtue to the ancient Stoics in achieving tranquility. Through self-discipline, one can master their emotions by pausing before reacting, thinking things through, and choosing actions wisely—ultimately attaining inner calm despite external chaos.

Developing self-discipline may be challenging at first, but engaging in consistent practice will greatly contribute to finding inner peace.

7. Engage with nature: Nature played a vital role in Stoic philosophy; they believed it offered solace, inspiration, and spiritual rejuvenation. Taking time to appreciate the beauty and serenity of the natural world can offer profound insights into human nature and a renewed connection with our surroundings.

Techniques for Managing Stress and Anxiety

Stress and anxiety are an inevitable part of life, but that doesn't mean they need to consume us. As stoics, we can learn to manage these emotions and find balance by using a blend of time-tested techniques and modern-day tools. Let's explore a few key strategies for managing stress and anxiety from a stoic perspective.

1. Cultivate mindfulness through meditation: Stress often arises from feeling overwhelmed by tasks and deadlines, or worrying about the future. One way to combat stress is through mindfulness—an approach to living in the present moment with awareness. By cultivating a mindfulness practice, such as meditation, we become better equipped at noticing when we're feeling stressed or anxious and can take steps to address those feelings.

The practice of meditation involves sitting quietly, focusing on your breath, and allowing thoughts to come and go without judgment or attachment. This helps build mental strength, resilience, and focus—key components of dealing with stress or anxiety effectively.

2. Reframe your thoughts: When you're experiencing stress or anxiety, it's common for our minds to jump to worst-case scenarios, leading to worry and rumination. In stoic philosophy, we are taught that our thoughts directly influence our emotions. Therefore, reframing negative thoughts can significantly impact how we feel and react.

For example, if you're stressed about an upcoming work presentation, instead of thinking "I'm going to fail," consider reframing the thought to "I will do my best." This shift in perspective reduces anxiety while still acknowledging the situation's challenges.

3. Practice acceptance: There will always be aspects of life that are beyond our control—honing our ability to accept what we can't change is critical in managing stress and anxiety from a stoic standpoint. We must recognize that certain things are not in our control (like other people's actions or world events) and develop a sense of inner peace despite external factors.

Practice accepting life's challenges as opportunities for growth, and focus on controlling your response to situations, rather than trying to control the circumstances themselves.

4. Identify your core values: Understanding what matters most to you can help create a sense of stability and purpose when facing stressful or anxiety-inducing situations. Take some time to reflect on your values and what you stand for, which can serve as an anchor during turbulent times.

By acting in alignment with your core values, you gain a sense of accomplishment and self-respect, making it easier to face challenges head-on without succumbing to stress or anxiety.

5. Engage in physical activity: It's well-known that exercise is an effective way to relieve stress—both in the short term and long term. The connection between mind and body is strong, and engaging in regular physical activity can bring numerous benefits, such as improved mood, better sleep quality, and reduced anxiety levels.

Find an activity that suits you—whether it's yoga, running, swimming, or simply going for a walk—and make it part of your self-care routine.

6. Seek social support: Humans are social creatures—we thrive on interaction and connection with others. Having a strong social support network can act as a buffer against stress. Surround yourself with people who are positive influences on your life and prioritize spending time with them. Share your worries with trusted friends or family members—they may offer new perspectives or solutions that you hadn't considered.

7. Prioritize self-care: In the stoic philosophy, self-care encompasses both physical and mental wellbeing—the two are intricately connected. Ensuring proper nutrition, adequate sleep, regular exercise, and engaging in activities that bring joy are essential components of overall well-being.

Regular self-care enables you to be more resilient in the face of stressors since it helps maintain a solid foundation of health both physically and mentally.

Stoic Meditation

Stoic meditation is a practice adapted from ancient Stoic philosophy, which places emphasis on self-control, personal virtue, and reflective thought. Stoicism encourages us to accept that which we cannot control and focus instead on cultivating our inner selves, particularly our thoughts and emotions. Meditation, in the context of Stoicism, is not merely a relaxation technique but a method to strengthen our minds and mold our character.

The following passage explores the core principles of Stoic meditation and provides guidance on how to incorporate these practices into your daily life. Through dedication and consistency, you may find these techniques helpful in fostering self-awareness, psychological resilience, and inner peace.

1. Mindfulness of Thoughts and Emotions: One of the foundational aspects of Stoic meditation is the awareness of one's own thoughts and emotions. Rather than being carried away by their power, the objective is to observe them from a distance. By doing so, we can prevent ourselves from falling prey to impulsive reactions or basing our judgments on irrational grounds.

To begin this practice, find a quiet space where you can sit comfortably without distractions. Close your eyes and direct your attention inward. As thoughts or emotions arise, simply observe their presence without judgment or engagement. While it may be tempting to dwell on certain ideas or feelings, remember that they are transient phenomena that do not shape your identity.

2. The Dichotomy of Control: The central tenet of Stoicism lies in recognizing the distinction between what we can control (our own actions) and what we cannot (external events). It teaches us to direct our focus solely towards actionable aspects of life.

Incorporate this idea into your meditation by contemplating the areas of your life over which you have influence. Connect with an empowering sense of agency that comes from focusing on things within your control while detaching from external factors beyond it.

3. Practicing Negative Visualization: Negative visualization is a Stoic technique that involves imagining negative scenarios or setbacks to cultivate emotional resilience. This practice allows us to mentally rehearse responding to adverse situations, fortifying us against potential stressors.

During your meditation session, envision yourself experiencing a challenging event, such as losing your job or receiving unpleasant news. Rather than succumbing to the fear or sorrow that may accompany these thoughts, reflect on how you might gracefully respond or adapt constructively. Through repeated practice, you can develop a deeper sense of courage and acceptance in the face of life's uncertainties.

4. Preparing for the Day with Premeditatio Malorum: Premeditatio malorum, or premeditating adversity, is another form of negative visualization tailored specifically to beginning each day with strengthened resolve. Early in the morning, take a few moments to meditate on potential struggles you might face throughout the day. By mentally rehearsing your response, you can better equip yourself to navigate these challenges with grace.

5. Evening Review: At the end of each day, engage in an evening review by reflecting on your actions and progress towards Stoic ideals.

Assess whether you practiced self-discipline and exhibited virtues like wisdom, courage, temperance, and justice.

Should you identify areas for improvement, contemplate how you can refine your thoughts and behavior going forward without dwelling on what cannot be undone. The purpose of this practice is not self-criticism but growth.

6. Developing Stoic Virtues: In addition to focusing on specific techniques, you can integrate overarching Stoic virtues into your meditation practice. For example:

- Cultivate wisdom by contemplating philosophical ideas or studying ancient texts,
- Strengthen courage through affirmations or mental imagery that reinforces determination,
- Develop temperance by deliberately choosing moderation over excess,
- Emphasize justice by considering the needs of others and aspiring towards fairness in your interactions.

Stoic meditation is not a one-size-fits-all procedure but rather a collection of practices aimed at fostering self-mastery, inner strength, and a deeper understanding of our place in the world. As you progress in your practice, you may find that certain techniques resonate more strongly with you while others do not. The goal is to create a personalized meditation routine that aligns with your own values and aspirations while staying true to the core principles of Stoicism.

Chapter 4

Building Resilience

Developing Emotional Strength

From social unrest to personal tragedies, it's becoming increasingly difficult for people to maintain emotional wellbeing. In these uncontrollable situations, developing emotional strength is paramount for lifelong resilience and unwavering contentment. The ancient philosophy of Stoicism offers practical tools to cultivate emotional strength and navigate the chaos of life with confidence. Developing emotional strength is a central tenet in the practice of Stoicism. As one progresses through life, they will undoubtedly face various challenges and trials that test their emotional resilience. By cultivating emotional strength, one can navigate through these difficult moments with grace and composure, allowing them to lead a more fulfilling and contented life.

At the core of developing emotional strength, lies the ability to acknowledge our emotions, understand their origin, and reframe their impact on our lives. Emotional strength is the capacity to withstand difficulties with grace and minimal distress. As we delve into the realm of Stoicism, we'll discover how to reclaim power over our emotions by harnessing rational thinking and focusing on what we can control.

External Circumstances vs. Internal Perceptions

A significant aspect of Stoicism lies in recognizing the distinction between external events beyond our control and our internal perception of those events. The only thing over which we truly possess control is our own thoughts, feelings, and reactions.

"Men are disturbed not by things, but by the views which they take of things." - Epictetus.

Developing emotional strength begins by recognizing that external circumstances themselves do not inherently elicit emotional responses in us; rather, it is our interpretation of those circumstances that ultimately determines how we feel. By adopting a stoic mindset, we learn to accept external events as indifferent – neither inherently good nor bad – instead focusing on how we internally process these situations.

Mindfulness & Self-Awareness

Being mindful of our thoughts and emotions is fundamental to developing emotional strength. By maintaining a conscious awareness of our thought patterns as they unfold during moments of adversity, we allow ourselves the opportunity to pause before reacting impulsively or emotionally.

This practice enables us to calmly assess situations from an unbiased standpoint rather than becoming overwhelmed by emotions such as anger or sadness. Over time, cultivating mindfulness allows us to better understand how our thoughts and emotions manifest in response to external events, empowering us to choose actions that reflect our principles and values.

Actively Strengthening Emotional Resilience

In addition to understanding the nature of our thoughts and emotions, developing emotional strength requires active effort. Stoicism encourages us to engage in reflection, self-scrutiny, and meditation as means of overcoming emotional hardships.

One effective technique in developing emotional resilience is the practice of negative visualization: imagining difficult scenarios or outcomes before they arise. By doing so, we learn to mentally prepare for potential difficulties, allowing us to confront them calmly when or if they actually arise. Additionally, negative visualization can instill a sense of gratitude and appreciation for what we currently have by contrasting it with less fortunate circumstances.

Another essential practice is remaining mindful of our values and principles during trying times. When faced with adversity, remind yourself of the morals and ideals that guide your life. This can help provide clarity amid emotional turmoil, giving you the strength and perspective necessary to remain composed despite external difficulties.

Techniques to Develop Emotional Strength

Stoic philosophers proposed numerous techniques to build emotional strength. Here are three practical approaches:

1. Contemplate Negative Outcomes: Rather than shying away from potential negative outcomes, Stoic practitioners suggest meditating on them to lessen their psychological impact. By preparing for setbacks in advance, you're more equipped to handle challenging circumstances.

2. Dichotomy of Control: Remember that there are things we can control and those we cannot. Focusing on what's within our control - such as our thoughts, emotions, and actions – enables us to minimize distractions and concentrate on self-improvement.

3. Voluntary Discomfort: Occasionally subjecting yourself to minor inconveniences can build mental endurance and help you appreciate daily comforts. This practice trains the mind to refrain from being overly attached to external factors.

Cultivating Emotional Strength in Everyday Life

Incorporating Stoic principles into your daily routine can aid in establishing emotional strength over time:

1. Maintain a morning meditation ritual where you envision possible challenges for the day and reflect on how you will respond rationally if confronted with adversity.
2. Practice journaling as a means to express your thoughts, analyze emotional triggers, and track progress.
3. Implement weekly voluntary discomfort exercises, such as fasting or taking cold showers, to train the mind's resilience.

The Path Towards Unshakable Resilience

Developing emotional strength is an ongoing process that takes conscious effort and consistent practice, yet its benefits are boundless. As you cultivate stoic virtues and apply their teachings in dealing with life's turbulence, you'll notice a profound shift towards personal resilience and unwavering equanimity.

By embracing the wisdom of Stoicism, you equip yourself with the mental fortitude necessary to weather any storm that life may throw at you. Ultimately, this philosophical journey leaves you with a deeper understanding of your emotions, the power of self-mastery, and the true essence of resilience.

Handling Adversity with Stoic Wisdom

In this section, we will address a fundamental topic in the practice of Stoicism: handling adversity. Adversity can take many forms, from everyday stress and frustrations to significant setbacks and life-altering challenges. But regardless of the scale or gravity of one's troubles, Stoicism offers an array of practical advice that can help us navigate life's trials with equanimity, resilience, and optimism.

The Gift of Perspective

One of the key tenets of Stoicism is that our suffering is rooted not in external events themselves, but in our interpretation of those events. As the

Stoic sage Epictetus famously remarked, "It is not things that disturb us, but our judgments about them." When faced with adversity, it's natural to focus on the harm or damage that we perceive as befalling us. But this habit of thought is precisely what exacerbates our distress.

Instead, Stoics seek to shift their perspective and reframe difficulties as opportunities for growth. They embrace hardship as an essential ingredient in personal development - a crucible in which they can cultivate virtues like patience, fortitude, and humility. By redirecting their attention away from their perceived misfortunes and onto the potential benefits therein, they gain a sense of agency and empowerment. Events that initially seemed painful or undesirable turn out to be disguised blessings.

Universal Interconnectedness

Another powerful Stoic insight is the recognition that we are all part of a vast interconnected web of existence - individual actors enmeshed within an intricate living tapestry. Our lives unfold according to an intricate divine plan; we each have a vital role to play in the common good. This cosmopolitan worldview instills a sense of humility in the face of adversity: it reminds us that we are but one small part of a vast cosmic drama.

By appreciating our place within the grand scheme of things, we realize that our adversities are but fleeting challenges that pale in comparison to the eternity of the universe. With this long-range cosmic perspective, our tribulations begin to dissolve into insignificance. They no longer have the power to unhinge us, and we can face them with equanimity.

Control vs. Influence

A key Stoic principle is that we should concern ourselves only with what lies within our control and accept what lies beyond it. To this end, Stoics adopt a crystal-clear distinction between things they genuinely control (their own thoughts, beliefs, attitudes) and external factors over which they have limited or no influence. When adversity strikes, we must direct our efforts towards those aspects of the situation that fall within our sphere of control:

our response to the crisis, how we manage our thoughts, emotions, and actions during the challenge. It's crucial to be honest with ourselves about where our true locus of control lies: not over outcomes, but in how we confront adversity and grow from it.

The Art of Practicing Misfortune

The Stoics were known for their commitment to practicing misfortune—deliberately immersing themselves in uncomfortable situations or voluntarily embracing hardship to foster resilience and gratitude. By incorporating adversity into their daily lives, they prepared themselves for actual difficulties when they arose. This practice can take many forms: spending some time in spartan conditions to appreciate the luxuries we often take for granted; purposely seeking out uncomfortable or challenging experiences like fasting or cold showers to remind ourselves of life's impermanence; or committing to tough physical exercise that chases away complacency and evokes a sense of accomplishment.

Compassion as a Remedy for Adversity

Just as important as cultivating inner strength is extending compassionate understanding towards others. In times of adversity, empathy can soothe emotional distress while also serving as a powerful tool for building relationships.

Stoics foster empathy by engaging in reflective exercises that invite us to step outside our perspectives and consider those of others. One often-cited practice is the "view from above," which consists of envisioning a bird's-eye view of the world to appreciate its diversity and remind ourselves of our shared human condition.

Adversity is an unavoidable aspect of the human experience, but its psychological impact is shaped by how we approach and manage it. Stoic wisdom provides essential guidance for facing life's challenges with grace and resilience.

Chapter 5

Cultivating Virtue

The Stoic Virtues: Wisdom, Courage, Justice, Temperance

Stoicism central tenets revolve around the cultivation of inner strength and finding contentment even in the most trying circumstances. At the heart of its teachings are four cardinal virtues, which Stoics believe should shape one's thoughts and actions:

1. Wisdom: Wisdom in Stoicism refers to practical wisdom – the ability to discern the best course of action based on a deep understanding of oneself and one's environment. This virtue is rooted in the pursuit of knowledge and a genuine love for truth. By nurturing wisdom, Stoics become adept at recognizing good from evil and distinguishing between what is within their control and what isn't.

Through the development of wisdom, a Stoic seeks to lead a purposeful life marked by thoughtfulness, mindfulness, and rationality. This often involves careful introspection as well as attentiveness to external factors. As the saying goes, "si vis pacem, para bellum" (if you want peace, be prepared for war). Wisdom involves being mentally prepared to navigate any potential challenge or adversity that life may present.

2. Courage: The hallmark of courage is the ability and willingness to face adversity head-on. In a Stoic context, this means not only confronting physical dangers but also confronting psychological or emotional challenges with resolve.

To possess courage does not signify recklessness. Instead, Stoics draw upon their inner strength and wisdom to determine when and how to confront obstacles with bravery. Seneca once wrote that true bravery is about "knowing what awaits him [and] calmly consenting to his fate." Practitioners learn to endure hardships with a sense of tranquility by reminding themselves that most obstacles are uncontrollable external factors.

3. Justice: Justice plays an essential role within Stoicism because it governs one's relationships with others, promoting fairness and harmonious interaction. It emphasizes empathy, compassion, and understanding for the well-being of society as a collective.

Just actions require treating others with respect and dignity, honoring personal commitments, and being willing to forgive. As Marcus Aurelius declared, "a wrong does not harm the agent so much... as it harms the doer." In other words, to act unjustly not only diminishes the well-being of others but also detracts from one's inner peace and self-respect.

True justice also involves recognizing wrongdoing and engaging in acts of benevolence when possible. By exhibiting just behavior, a Stoic manifests an honorable character that earns the respect of others – a virtue crucial to both personal growth and social harmony.

4. Temperance: Temperance is synonymous with moderation in Stoicism. It implies a sense of reasoned self-restraint that allows individuals to avoid excess or indulgence. Desire, according to Stoic teaching, can lead to emotional turmoil which clouds judgment and undermines wisdom.

By practicing temperance, one cultivates the ability to control impulses related to anger, desire, envy, or fear. Although the goal is not abstention from everything pleasurable or difficult emotions entirely, it involves finding balance in all aspects of life.

Achieving temperance includes monitoring one's thoughts and actions. This deliberate self-awareness fosters healthy habits conducive to maintaining a clear-minded perspective. Under this mindful approach, success becomes achievable without spiraling into egoism and failure breeds emotional resilience rather than despair.

The Communion of Virtues

Taken together, these four virtues form the ethical foundation upon which Stoicism is built. Like threads woven into a tapestry, each virtue reinforces the other; wisdom cannot truly exist without courage since wisdom must be applied even during adversity. Similarly, courage without justice may lead to reckless behavior that disregards others' well-being.

It is important to remember that for Stoics, these virtues are not dogmatic commandments but rather principles to guide a fulfilling life. As one engages with each virtue, they strive towards achieving inner peace (ataraxia) and tranquility, which are the core aims of Stoicism.

Practicing Virtue in Daily Life

Incorporating the four cardinal virtues of Stoicism - wisdom, courage, justice, and temperance - into our daily lives is an ongoing process that requires self-awareness and conscious effort. By cultivating these virtues, we develop a strong foundation upon which to build a contented and purposeful life. The following strategies will aid in the practical application of Stoic principles in various spheres of our everyday existence:

1. Morning reflection: Start each day with a period of contemplation, focusing on the virtues you wish to cultivate. Envision your day ahead, and mentally rehearse how you will embody wisdom, courage, justice, and temperance in various situations. By doing so, you prime yourself to act with virtue throughout the day.

2. Focus on what's within your control: Mindfully distinguish between what is within your control and what is not when confronting challenges or making decisions. Recognize that external circumstances may not always be influenceable; instead, prioritize your own thoughts, actions, and responses – factors under your direct control.

3. Practice mindful decision-making: As you face decisions throughout the day, pause to reflect on the virtuous course of action. Consider how different options align with wisdom, courage, justice, and temperance before making choices that reflect your commitment to living a Stoic life.

4. Pause before responding: When confronted with emotionally charged situations or conflicts, practice the art of pausing before reacting. This allows you to gain perspective and assess your thoughts and emotions from a place of reason rather than impulsivity. Make sure that your response aligns with the Stoic virtues before acting.

5. Cultivate gratitude: Regularly express gratitude for the positive aspects of your life and for any obstacles that provide opportunities for growth. By focusing on what you have rather than what you lack or desire, you develop contentment and foster temperance.

6. Engage in introspection: Set aside time each day for self-reflection and introspection. Assess your actions, thoughts, and habits against the Stoic virtues of wisdom, courage, justice, and temperance. Be honest with yourself about areas for improvement and commit to cultivating those virtues moving forward.

7. Evening review: At the close of each day, take the time to evaluate your daily actions and thoughts concerning the Stoic virtues. Acknowledge your successes in maintaining virtuous behavior, identify areas that require improvement, and assess your progress on the path to embodying Stoicism fully.

8. Surround yourself with like-minded individuals: Building relationships with individuals who share similar values or who are also working on cultivating Stoic virtues can provide encouragement, accountability, and support on your journey.

9. Contribute to others: Seek opportunities to contribute positively to the lives of those around you. Acts of kindness and compassion not only strengthen your commitment to justice but also foster meaningful connections within your community.

10. Embrace obstacles as opportunities for growth: Rather than viewing adversities as setbacks or sources of frustration, adopt a Stoic mindset that sees obstacles as chances to learn, grow, and demonstrate virtue. Each challenge encountered is an opportunity for further development along the path of becoming a fully realized Stoic practitioner.

By actively practicing these strategies in daily life, you will gradually ingrain the cardinal virtues into your character, thus embodying the essence of Stoicism. Remember, personal transformation is a lifelong journey – stay committed to continuous growth and self-improvement as you apply these principles day by day. Through steadfast dedication, you'll find tranquility and contentment in even the most challenging circumstances as you embrace the timeless wisdom of Stoicism.

Part 3: Stoicism In Relationships

As you continue your study of Stoicism in Part 3, you'll see how this ancient philosophy can not only serve as a guide for personal growth but can bring out the best in our relationships. We explore the application of Stoic principles in friendships, family interactions and conflict resolution. Additionally, we consider the influence of Stoicism on parenting—teaching you how to raise virtuous children imbued with stoic values and instilling stoic resilience within them to better navigate the challenges they face throughout life.

Chapter 6

Stoic Relationships

Stoic relationships form the cornerstone of the Stoicism Bible's teachings, acknowledging our deep interconnectedness and interdependence as human beings. A core aspect of Stoicism lies in understanding that while we cannot control external events or the behavior of others, we can control our reactions and responses to them. In this chapter, we explore how stoic principles can be applied to building and nurturing meaningful, life-affirming relationships.

Stoics prioritize equanimity, courage, wisdom, and justice - traits that serve as strong foundations for healthy relationships. To foster these characteristics within ourselves and our partnerships, we must first examine key concepts of Stoic philosophy that guide our interactions:

1. The Dichotomy of Control: Inherent within every relationship is the dichotomy of control - recognizing that we only have direct influence over our own thoughts, emotions, and actions. Accepting this fact liberates us from the emotional turmoil caused by attempting to manipulate or control others. Instead, focusing on what lies within our power cultivates inner growth and harmony.

2. Practicing Empathy: Embracing empathy enables us to view situations from another person's perspective, fostering understanding and compassion. Remember Marcus Aurelius' timeless words: "Whenever you are about to find fault with someone, ask yourself the following question: What fault of mine most nearly resembles the one I am about to criticize?" By turning this critical lens upon ourselves first, we approach others with humility.

3. Embracing Amor Fati: As Zeno, the founder of Stoicism wrote, "Fate leads the willing and drags along the unwilling." The principle of amor fati captures the essence of wholeheartedly accepting life's circumstances - not just tolerating them but loving them as an integral part of our existence. Applying amor fati in relationships encourages resilience and adaptability through fluctuating circumstances.

4. Memento Mori: The practice of memento mori reminds us of life's impermanence and the inevitability of death. Mindfulness of this fact allows us to appreciate and cherish our time with our loved ones, fostering conscious, purposeful connections and prioritizing the essential over the trivial.

Now that we understand these foundational principles, let's apply them to the dynamics within stoic relationships:

Cultivating Friendships: Friendships forged upon stoic ideals consist of mutual admiration for each other's virtues and shared commitment to personal growth. Stoic friends act as mirrors, reflecting back an objective account of our actions and intentions. Endeavor to be honest, loyal, and compassionate in your friendships, offering gentle guidance rather than unsolicited advice.

Romantic Partnerships: Romantic love holds a special place within the stoic framework due to its deep emotional significance. Rather than getting swayed by passionate desires or possessiveness, approach romantic relationships with a sense of equanimity grounded in logic and reason. Uphold trustworthiness, loyalty, and respect as cornerstones while maintaining a sense of individuality.

Family Dynamics: In our relationships with parents, siblings, and extended family members, an appreciation of the inherent randomness of fate is crucial. Remember that familial bonds result from a complex interplay of circumstances beyond our control. Accepting familial obligations while upholding moral integrity provides a basis for nurturing deep connections within this sphere.

Professional Relationships: In professional settings, it is crucial to maintain level-headedness and prioritize ethical behavior above personal gain. Exercise humility in acknowledging your limitations and seek teamwork to achieve shared goals. Utilize stoic wisdom in navigating conflicts or misunderstandings without letting emotions overrule reason.

Community and Beyond: Our role in society extends beyond just those we consider family or friends; we are part of an intricate web connecting fellow human beings with diverse backgrounds and experiences. Embrace unity and strive towards contributing positively to your community. In the words of Seneca: "We are waves of the same sea, leaves of the same tree, flowers of the same garden."

Applying Stoicism to Friendships and Family

In the previous chapters, we have explored the fundamental principles of Stoicism and how they can be applied in various aspects of life. In this section, we will delve into the art of maintaining harmonious relationships with friends and family through the lens of Stoicism.

To attain harmony in our relationships with those closest to us, it is essential to implement the four cardinal virtues of Stoicism—wisdom, courage, justice, and temperance. Let us explore how each virtue can contribute to the growth and strength of our bonds with friends and family.

1. Wisdom: The ability to discern what is within our control and what isn't is a key aspect of Stoic wisdom. Recognizing that other people's thoughts, feelings, and actions lie outside our control can help maintain peace within our relationships.

By focusing on our own thoughts and reactions, we can cultivate better communication skills and avoid unnecessary conflicts. For example, when faced with a disagreement between you and your friend or family member on religion or politics, instead of insisting on being right or trying to change their opinion, navigate the conversation respectfully while staying open to different perspectives. This practice will not only create an environment for open dialogue but also strengthen your bond by valuing mutual respect.

2. Courage: Courage in relationships is about facing emotional challenges with steadfastness and determination instead of avoiding them out of fear or discomfort. Embracing vulnerability while supporting one another can fortify trust among friends and family members. Be willing to share your feelings openly without fear of judgment or ridicule—this honesty will signal to your loved ones that you are genuine and invested in their well-being.

Addressing conflicts with courage also entails standing up for your values and principles when necessary. While Stoicism underlines the value of tolerance and understanding, it is crucial to communicate your boundaries assertively without sacrificing your moral compass.

3. Justice: Treating friends and family with fairness, kindness, and respect forms the cornerstone of just relationships. Show appreciation for their efforts, be patient in times of stress, and lend a helping hand during difficult moments.

In the pursuit of justice, avoid gossiping or speaking ill of others when they are not present. This practice will create a sense of security within your circle, knowing that you are trustworthy and loyal to your connections.

4. Temperance: Exercising self-control is essential for maintaining balance in our relationships. By demonstrating restraint over our words, emotions, and actions, we can foster an atmosphere of respect and understanding among loved ones.

Reflect on how you react to irritations within your relationships—are you quick to anger or frustration? Before responding impulsively to a provocation or argument, take a step back and remember the Stoic principle of focusing on situations within your control instead of reacting with baseless emotion. This practice can help maintain harmony between you and those close to you.

As humans evolve over time, so do our relationships—requiring us to adapt accordingly. Stoicism provides useful tools for navigating these changes while nurturing strong connections with friends and family. By embodying the virtues mentioned earlier as we face personal growth, societal shifts, distance, or even loss, we build resilience within ourselves and our relationships.

Resolving Conflicts Stoically

Disagreements arise due to contrasting viewpoints, misunderstandings, and clashes in values or interests. However, Stoicism, an ancient philosophy rooted in logic and rationality, presents itself as an effective approach for resolving conflicts in a calm and composed manner. The core principle of Stoicism encourages individuals to focus on what they can control and accept what they cannot. By applying this perspective to conflict resolution, we create a path toward mutual understanding and foster harmonious relationships.

To resolve conflicts stoically, we must first examine the foundational principles that underlie this philosophy. The Four Cardinal Virtues serve as pillars for maintaining a stoic mindset in the face of adversity. These virtues guide our hearts and minds when we encounter interpersonal struggles.

The following practical steps will enable you to embrace these virtues when faced with a conflict:

1. Recognize your emotions: Reflect on your emotional state and work towards composing yourself before engaging in any form of resolution. Be honest about the root causes of your emotions and how they could influence your perception of the situation.

2. Practice empathy: To resolve conflicts stoically, it is crucial to understand the perspectives of all involved parties. Put yourself in their shoes and muster compassion toward their emotional experiences.

3. Identify common ground: Look for shared values or mutual interests that can serve as a foundation for negotiation. Identifying commonalities will make it easier to find a solution that satisfies both parties.

4. Communicate openly and honestly: Effective communication, void of impulsive reactions and destructive language, is key to resolving conflicts with a stoic mindset. Adopt active listening skills, share your thoughts assertively but respectfully, and avoid taking disagreements personally.

5. Cultivate patience: Respect the time it takes for others to gather their thoughts, process emotions, and reach a resolution. Patience is not only a virtue but also an essential aspect of conflict resolution.

6. Seek outside help if necessary: Sometimes the severity or complexity of a conflict necessitates assistance from an impartial third party who can guide discussions and ensure that all parties are heard objectively. Don't hesitate to seek counseling or mediation if needed.

7. Accept the outcome: Once you've made your best effort to resolve the conflict in accordance with stoic principles, accept the outcome gracefully even if it's not entirely favorable to you.

Living in harmony with others remains an ideal we must continually strive toward despite our inherent human differences. Practicing Stoicism encourages us to approach these conflicts rationally and comfortably, focusing on what we can control without letting external circumstances dictate our inner peace.

Chapter 7

Stoic Parenting

Many parents turn to Stoicism as a guiding philosophy to instill the skills, knowledge, and resilience needed to thrive in an era of excess and distraction. With its focus on wisdom, courage, justice, and temperance, Stoicism can provide the foundation for a successful approach to parenting that elevates our children's ability to navigate life effectively.

1. Wisdom: One of the core virtues of Stoicism is the pursuit of wisdom – the ability to discern what truly matters amidst all life's distractions and uncertainties. As parents, imparting wisdom means teaching children critical thinking skills and guiding them towards truth and understanding.

1. Encourage curiosity: Embrace your child's inquisitive nature by fostering their curiosity about the world around them. Emphasize the importance of asking questions and seeking answers through research, analysis, and reflection.
2. Teach problem-solving: Stress the need for logic-based solutions by engaging with your kids in conversations or exercises that challenge them to think rationally about any given situation.

3. Model humility: Remember that mistakes are part of the learning process. Apologize when necessary so your child understands that no one is infallible.

2. Courage: Fostering courage in today's age might seem like an uphill battle given societal norms that reward instant gratification, material possessions, and superficiality. Still, simple daily practices can help instill courage in your children.

1. *Embrace hardships:* Teach kids about adversity as a natural part of life and an essential component of growth rather than something to be feared or avoided.
2. *Develop emotional regulation:* Guide them through managing their negative emotions, like anger, fear, and frustration, in a healthy manner, as Stoics have done for centuries.
3. *Encourage risk-taking:* Demonstrate to your kids the importance of thoughtful risk-taking as a productive method to broaden their horizons and overcome adversity.

3. Justice: In a world where injustice often goes unnoticed or even normalized, it's crucial to teach our children to act fairly and ethically driven by the Stoic virtue of justice.

1. *Educate about compassion:* Emphasize the importance of empathy and kindness. It is essential to help kids understand that every individual and living being deserves respect and dignity.
2. *Teach moral reasoning:* Encourage them to make ethical choices driven by principles and encourage open discussions around what is right or wrong in various situations.
3. *Reinforce fairness in daily interactions:* Objectively show your kids how their actions affect others by setting boundaries and holding them accountable for their behavior.

4. Temperance: Teaching temperance requires a delicate balance between offering guidance and modeling self-control, as it is central to achieving emotional tranquility in both children's and parents' lives.

1. *Develop self-discipline*: Help kids understand the power of delayed gratification through responsibilities like chores or long-term projects which demonstrate that short-term sacrifices can lead to long-term rewards.
2. *Cultivate mindfulness:* Guide your child towards mindfulness practices such as deep breathing or meditation which offers benefits like better stress management and improved mental clarity.
3. *Set healthy life patterns:* Promote healthy habits from an early age, encompassing various aspects like exercise, nutrition, sleep hygiene, and digital device usage to help them achieve mental and physical balance on their journey into adulthood.

Following these four virtues is just the initial step; incorporating daily Stoic practices can fortify parenting efforts in the long run:

1. *Remember your control:* Focus on things within your control while recognizing that some outcomes are beyond your influence. Focus on guiding your children based on Stoic principles while allowing them to grow and learn within their sphere of control.
2. *Reflect on gratitude*: Share moments of gratitude daily, discussing the goodness and value in simplicity – an essential tenant of Stoic teachings.
3. *Cultivate resilience:* Be a reliable, consistent, and approachable figure in your child's life, and encourage them to confront the future with determination and courage.

Raising Virtuous Children with Stoic Values

The ancient school of Stoicism teaches us that virtue is the ultimate good and that our ability to reason and act ethically is what differentiates us from other creatures. In today's world, when cultural values seem to waver with every passing trend, it is crucial for parents to instill in their children a strong moral compass built on the firm foundation of Stoic values.

Raising virtuous children in our turbulent times may feel like a Herculean task. However, by following the core principles of Stoicism, parents can nurture a life-long love for wisdom, self-discipline, and emotional resilience in their children.

1. Teach your children the value of wisdom: Wisdom lies at the heart of Stoicism. It means understanding that some things are within our control, like our thoughts and emotions, while others are not. Encourage your child to differentiate between these two spheres and to focus on improving what they can control.

You can guide your child towards wisdom by helping them navigate everyday challenges in a reflective manner. Ask questions that prompt critical thinking about their actions and beliefs while encouraging an open discussion that fosters cognitive growth.

2. Build self-discipline through consistent practice: Stoicism emphasizes discipline in one's thoughts, actions, and emotions. These qualities won't simply present themselves out of thin air – they require continuous effort to cultivate. Parents can help establish healthy habits by enforcing regular routines around essential aspects of daily life such as sleep, diet, physical activity, and study.

Providing structure and promoting consistency sets a positive example for your child that self-discipline lays the groundwork for success in all areas of life.

3. Foster emotional resilience: The ebb and flow of emotions are an inevitable aspect of human existence. However, Stoic philosophy empowers individuals to maintain composure even amid adversity by separating external events from personal reactions.

When your child faces difficult situations, resist the urge to indulge their negative emotions. Instead, use these moments as opportunities to teach them valuable coping skills. By showing your children how to identify and manage their emotions, they will be better equipped to handle life's challenges with grace and poise.

4. Encourage acts of kindness and empathy: In Marcus Aurelius's Meditations, he reminds us that we are all in this world together and must learn to work for one another's benefit. Emphasize to your children the value of empathy and kindness through acts of generosity, volunteer work, or simply being a supportive friend.

When children witness their own ability to make a difference in someone else's life, it strengthens their sense of purpose and helps them understand that true virtue extends beyond the self.

5. Nurture a love for learning: The Stoics believed that cultivating knowledge was an essential part of the pursuit of virtue. As a parent, you can foster this love of learning by continually encouraging your child to pursue knowledge in various areas – from history to science, literature to art.

Moreover, exposing your child to Stoic philosophy will deepen their appreciation for reason and intellectual development while broadening their perspectives on personal growth.

6. Lead by example: Teaching your child about Stoic values is only half the battle – being a living embodiment of those principles is equally crucial. Set an example for your child by striving for calmness amid chaos; opting for rationality over impulsivity; demonstrating patience and persistence when facing obstacles; and offering kindness even when it is challenging to do so.

7. Stay patient: Rome wasn't built in a day; neither will virtuous individuals emerge overnight. Raising virtuous children with Stoic values takes time, effort, and patience. Be gentle with yourself and your child during this journey, remembering that even the great Stoic philosophers were once children who too needed guidance.

As a parent, you have the immense responsibility of shaping your child's character and helping them become ethical, resilient individuals. By incorporating the timeless wisdom of Stoic philosophy into the fabric of everyday life, you can empower your child to lead a life grounded in virtue, no matter what challenges they may face.

Instilling Stoic Resilience in Kids

As parents or caregivers, one of our primary goals should be to instill this sense of resilience in our children so they can grow into strong, emotionally intelligent adults. Let's delve into practical ways by which parents can imbue their children with the essential values of Stoicism, ultimately building their resilience and equipping them to confront life's many challenges.

1. Emphasize the importance of self-control: Self-control is a cornerstone of stoic teaching; it focuses on decision-making and emotional mastery. Encourage your child to recognize and understand their emotions instead of suppressing them. Offer guidance by teaching techniques such as pausing before reacting and engaging in deep-breathing exercises.

2. Teach the differentiation between external events and one's reactions: Stoicism emphasizes that while we can't control external events, we can indeed control how we respond to them. Teach your kids this critical difference early on, helping them realize that their happiness is not dictated by exterior factors but rather by their interpretation of these events.

3. Emphasizing Self-Awareness: Stoicism teaches that self-awareness is the foundation of personal growth and development. By helping children become aware of their thoughts and feelings, we can encourage them to recognize their agency in shaping their responses to different situations.

One way to promote self-awareness is through regular check-ins with your child, asking questions about their emotions, thoughts, and experiences. This practice encourages introspection and creates an open dialogue between you and your child, fostering trust.

Another effective tool for self-awareness is journaling. Encourage your child to keep a daily journal or diary, where they can write down their thoughts, emotions, and experiences. This helps them develop critical thinking skills and better understand themselves.

4. Encouraging Rational Thinking: Stoicism emphasizes logic and reason as integral components of a resilient mindset. By teaching children to think rationally about their problems, we help them devise solutions that make the most sense for their situation.

One way to encourage rational thinking is by discussing hypothetical scenarios with your child – these can be real-life situations they may face or imaginative scenarios you create together. Help them analyze each situation by asking guiding questions like:

- What should be the goal in this situation?
- What are the potential obstacles?
- What steps can you take to reach the goal?

Another helpful method is to introduce them to Socratic questioning, which is based on the teaching style of the ancient Greek philosopher Socrates. In this method, you ask questions to challenge your child's assumptions and encourage them to reach conclusions through logical reasoning.

5. Introduce Mindfulness and Reflection: A Stoic practice that greatly enhances mental resilience is mindfulness – being fully aware of one's thoughts and emotions in any given moment. This awareness allows us to recognize negative emotions and temper our reactions to difficult circumstances.

To nurture mindfulness in your child, introduce them to basic meditation practices that focus on breathing and bodily sensations. Another method is to encourage them to pause throughout the day – perhaps during a difficult task or after a disagreement – and reflect on their emotions without judgment.

Instilling Stoic resilience in kids not only helps them navigate life's challenges with grace but also lays the groundwork for a meaningful and virtuous life. Through self-awareness, rational thinking, acceptance, virtue, and mindfulness, we can empower our children to become resilient individuals guided by the wisdom of Stoicism.

6. Expose them to adversity – safely: One of the best ways for kids to develop resilience is through controlled exposure to adversity. By facing challenges head-on – within safe parameters – children learn how to cope with stressors effectively. Of course, this doesn't mean placing your child in harm's way. Instead, allow them to experience manageable difficulties like trying new sports, solving complex puzzles, or learning new skills.

7. Emphasize the value of perseverance: It is essential to encourage children to go beyond their limits and push through challenges with determination – an integral part of Stoic resilience. Teach your child the importance of perseverance by providing examples from history or your own life experiences.

8. Foster a growth mindset: Nurturing resilience in children is incomplete without fostering a growth mindset – the belief that abilities and intelligence can be developed with hard work and determination. Teach your child to view failures as opportunities for growth, rather than setbacks to be avoided. Encourage them to embrace the journey of self-improvement continually.

9. Model Stoic behaviors yourself: As a parent, you are the most influential teacher in your child's life. To instill Stoic resilience in your kids, ensure that you model such behavior yourself – practice self-control, differentiate between external events and inner reactions, reflect on your experiences, persevere through challenges, and consistently display a growth-focused mentality.

10. Equip them with practical Stoic exercises: Incorporate activities into your daily routine that resonate with stoic teachings; for example:

1. *Negative visualization:* Have your child imagine worst-case scenarios and how they would deal with them effectively.

2. *Virtue identification:* Encourage your child to identify strengths exhibited by people they interact with daily and discuss how they can nurture those qualities within themselves.
3. *Contemplating impermanence:* Teach children to appreciate the transient nature of life, prompting gratitude for what they have.

11. Incorporate stories or biographies of prominent Stoics: To mold resilient kids using stoicism principles, it's helpful to expose them to notable figures who have embodied these teachings throughout history – people like Seneca, Epictetus, or Marcus Aurelius. Use relevant stories or biographies to demonstrate how Stoic resilience allowed them to persevere during challenging times, and how their teachings continue to inspire countless individuals today.

12. Nurture supportive relationships & community: Finally, fostering a sense of togetherness and connectedness among family members or peers is paramount to creating an environment that breeds resilience. Surround your child with like-minded individuals who share a commitment to self-improvement, empathy, and stoicism's principled way of life.

Part 4: Stoicism In The Modern World

In Part 4, we dive into the practical applications of Stoicism in today's fast-paced society. Discover how workplace dynamics can be transformed by embracing Stoic leadership and problem-solving strategies. Learn how Stoic ethics can inspire social responsibility and motivate individuals to become agents of positive change in the world.

Chapter 8

Stoicism in the Workplace

Emperor Marcus Aurelius, one of the most famous Stoic philosophers, once said, "If someone tries to unsettle your composure—don't let your mind be agitated. The key is to keep returning to focus on what is right and act accordingly." This quote sets the tone for this chapter as we delve into the application of Stoicism in the workplace and how it can lead to a more contented and productive professional experience.

Work is an essential part of our lives. It provides us with a means to meet our basic needs and allows us to develop personal skills. In today's fast-paced world, professionals face constant challenges that can generate significant stress, result in emotional turmoil, or cloud our judgment. This is where Stoicism comes into play. By adopting the principles of Stoic philosophy in our professional lives, we can achieve inner peace and become more effective at work.

1. Understanding what you control: The first step towards implementing Stoicism at work is understanding the concept of control. As human beings, we often desire a sense of autonomy over our circumstances; however, not everything will be under our control. Rather than stressing about situations that are beyond our reach, Stoicism teaches us to focus on that which we can control. For instance, you cannot control other peoples' actions but can choose how you respond to their behavior.

2. Keeping emotions in check: Negative emotions such as anger, frustration, anxiety, and envy are common in the workplace. The Stoic practice involves reflecting on our reactions to external events—whether positive or negative—and finding an appropriate response based on logic rather than emotions. Anger may cloud your judgment and hinder problem-solving skills; instead of letting it consume you, try detaching from situations that trigger these emotions so you remain clear-headed and focused.

3. Accepting change and adapting: Stoicism teaches us that change is inevitable, and it is our responsibility to adapt to new circumstances. In the workplace, this may mean welcoming new team members, adjusting to shifting roles, or embracing evolving industry trends. Embracing change equips us with resilience, enabling us to handle uncertainty with grace.

4. The power of perspective: One of the main elements of Stoic philosophy is adopting a different perspective on challenges and setbacks. When things do not go as planned at work, it's crucial to view obstacles as opportunities for growth and learning. Mistakes are inevitable; accepting them and drawing useful lessons can help us become more resilient and adaptive in the future.

5. Focusing on virtues: Stoicism places great importance on living a virtuous life. When it comes to the workplace, embodying virtues such as wisdom, courage, temperance, and justice will contribute to your overall well-being and professional development. Wisdom enables you to make sound decisions; courage allows you to face obstacles head-on; temperance teaches self-control; while justice encourages fairness and empathy for others.

6. The value of reflection: Taking time for self-reflection is an essential element in developing a Stoic mindset. A common Stoic practice involves setting aside time each day for self-examination—identifying aspects of your behavior that align with your values and those that might require adjustment. Reflecting on work experiences will improve decision-making abilities, enhance emotional intelligence, and ultimately lead to a more balanced professional life.

7. Remaining focused: Instead of worrying about what's on other peoples' plates or gossip-filled office chatter, maintaining focus on specific goals ensures consistent productivity regardless of external influences. Concentrate on meaningful tasks that are under your control and know when to let go of inconsequential distractions.

By adopting Stoicism's principles in the workplace, you can develop resilience in high-pressure situations while cultivating rational responses to stressors and negative emotions that arise during daily encounters. Furthermore, embracing change, valuing reflection, and focusing on virtues ensure a well-balanced, gratifying professional journey.

Becoming a Stoic Leader

Workplaces today are filled with challenging situations, unforeseen obstacles, and inevitable conflicts. Many leaders are beginning to recognize that personal and professional success may be deeply intertwined with how well they can practice stoicism in their day-to-day professional lives.

Stoicism emphasizes the cultivation of virtue and wisdom, focusing on maintaining a tranquil mindset amidst the chaos of external circumstances. As leaders adopt the principles of stoicism in their professional lives, they can cultivate inner strength, resilience, and self-discipline to thrive in any challenging environment. In this section, we will explore stoic principles that can serve as pillars for leadership in the modern workplace:

1. Cultivating Virtue as a Guiding Light: For a stoic leader, virtues such as wisdom, courage, justice, and temperance should be central to their decision-making process. By fostering a strong moral compass driven by virtues instead of personal interests or short-term gains, leaders can navigate complex situations more effectively.

In the context of the workplace, leaders might face various ethical dilemmas or challenging interpersonal conflicts. By focusing on virtues such as honesty, fairness, and empathy during these critical moments, stoic leaders can prioritize ethical actions above all else and earn the trust and respect of those around them.

2. Control What is Within Your Control: In any workplace scenario, there will be things entirely within your control (e.g., planning processes), things partially within your control (e.g., team efficiency), and things outside of your control (e.g., market conditions). Recognition of this simple truth can make the job environment less stressful and more manageable.

A leader who can identify and focus on their sphere of control can avoid becoming distracted or overwhelmed by things they cannot change. Leaders should direct their energy towards improving processes, supporting team members, and bolstering resources while letting go of uncontrollable factors od the environment.

3. Embrace Adversity and Challenge: Obstacles are not only inevitable but also a source of growth. The stoic leader perceives challenges as opportunities to learn, refine strategies, and become stronger professionally and personally.

When facing adversity or setbacks in the workplace, such as missed deadlines or dissatisfied clients, leaders who approach these situations with a stoic mindset will be better equipped to maintain composure and adapt effectively. By finding lessons in obstacles and maintaining a positive outlook, leaders can inspire team members to display resilience and determination in the face of challenges.

4. Practicing Mindful Reflection: Stoicism encourages introspection and self-analysis as pathways towards self-improvement. Leaders should make time for thoughtful reflection on their experiences, decisions, emotions, and reactions to gain valuable insights into their leadership style.

By identifying patterns of behavior that might be hindering professional development or preventing effective communication with colleagues, the stoic leader can take the necessary steps to modify their approach for optimal results.

While individual practice of stoicism can benefit any leader in the workplace holistically, fostering a culture that encourages stoicism throughout the organization can lead to even stronger benefits.

Promoting a culture based on stoic principles helps create an environment where employees feel safe expressing concerns, engaging in open dialogue, taking responsibility for their actions willingly, and embracing growth through challenges. By sharing these principles with others in your organization—through coaching sessions or team-building activities—you'll expand the circle of positive influence as your team members also reap the benefits of practicing stoicism.

Stoic Problem-Solving at Work

The ancient philosophy of Stoicism offers practical guidance for navigating the complexities of work and building a foundation to take on problems with rationality, clarity, and equanimity. Let's explore the guiding principles of Stoic problem-solving at work and how you can apply them to the challenges you may encounter in your professional life.

1. Embrace Obstacles as Opportunities: The first step in adopting a Stoic mindset towards problem-solving is to view obstacles not as hindrances, but as opportunities for growth. This principle is derived from the famous quote from Seneca, "Difficulties strengthen the mind, as labor does the body." As you face adversity at work, consider how it can provide lessons that will ultimately make you stronger and more capable.

To do this, remind yourself that struggling is part of the process of improving professionally. When faced with a challenging task or frustrating situation, focus not on the problem itself but on how overcoming it will help you grow in your career.

2. Distinguish Between What You Can Control and What You Cannot: A core tenet of Stoicism involves recognizing the difference between what is within your power to control and what is not. By doing so, you can direct your energy and resources towards addressing issues that are within your sphere of influence rather than becoming bogged down by external factors beyond your reach.

At work, it is crucial to focus on solutions that are actionable and within your domain. Instead of wasting time worrying about problems outside your purview or attempting to change others' behavior or opinions, concentrate solely on what you can achieve independently.

3. Maintain Composure Under Pressure: Maintaining emotional balance when dealing with challenging situations is perhaps one of the most valuable skills cultivated through Stoicism. By staying calm and level-headed, you are more likely to make rational decisions and avoid succumbing to the turbulence of emotions such as anger, frustration, or fear.

In the workplace, practice maintaining composure by taking regular breaks to reflect and reset, especially during high-pressure situations. Use deep-breathing techniques, mindfulness exercises, or simply take a short walk to remove yourself from the source of stress temporarily and regain control of your emotions.

4. Reframe Your Perspective: When encountering adversity at work, it is helpful to reframe situations to gain a fresh perspective. The Stoic practice of negative visualization can be used here to envision the worst-case scenario, which may ultimately make the actual problem seem less significant.

For instance, if faced with a difficult project deadline approaching, imagine not meeting the deadline and contemplate the subsequent potential consequences. Upon examining that extreme outcome, you may realize that while failure is not desirable, it is also not the end of your professional world. This mental exercise can help you better prioritize your approach to solving the problem at hand.

5. Seek Wise Counsel: Stoicism emphasizes seeking wisdom from both oneself and others when grappling with difficulties. At work, consider turning to colleagues or mentors for guidance and support in addressing your challenges. By engaging in open and candid conversations about your struggles with trusted individuals, you can gain valuable insights that may help you formulate effective solutions.

Additionally, remember that seeking assistance is not a sign of weakness; rather, it indicates a strong willingness to learn from others' experiences and enhance your own knowledge. Be humble enough to ask for help when necessary.

6. Cultivate Resilience Through Reflective Practices: Lastly, instilling resilience in dealing with workplace challenges requires consistent self-reflection. Regularly assessing your actions and thought processes allows for personal growth and understanding of how best to handle adversity moving forward.

Engage in reflective practices such as journaling or meditation; these activities can help you break down your experiences with workplace challenges, identify patterns, and formulate strategies for future improvement.

Chapter 9

Stoicism and Social Impact

Stoicism has an enduring impact on social dynamics since its inception. Known for its emphasis on rational thinking, self-discipline, and emotional resilience, Stoicism has profoundly shaped the way people engage with their environments and experience the world around them. In this chapter, we will explore the concept of Stoicism in terms of its social implications and discover how it has been interwoven with various aspects of life throughout history.

The fundamental principles of Stoicism assert that individuals must strive for equanimity and inner peace by learning to control their emotions, desires, and judgments. Through this process of self-examination and emotional regulation, one can cultivate a sense of harmony and balance within themselves and their social surroundings. This tenet is based on the belief that external circumstances are beyond our control, but our internal responses to these situations are within our grasp.

The stoic perspective encourages practitioners to maintain a strong ethical compass that informs their actions in every aspect of life. Rooted in virtue ethics, it advocates for understanding one's duties as part of a harmonious whole in society while acknowledging the interconnectedness that exists between all beings. By cultivating virtues such as wisdom, courage, justice, and temperance, Stoics believe they can both enrich their personal lives and make meaningful contributions to their communities.

As an influential philosophy throughout history, Stoicism has shaped various aspects of society from the fabric of political institutions to interpersonal relationships. World leaders like Marcus Aurelius and Seneca professed their understanding of Stoic precepts in their writings which reflected their adherence to the principles in their governance. The tenets have indeed infiltrated political discourse over time and continued to influence decision-making processes at various junctures in world history.

In interpersonal relationships too, Stoicism provides valuable guidance on managing one's emotions and practicing empathy. It encourages people to listen attentively, validate others' feelings and experiences even if they do not agree with them, and respond with kindness and understanding. By emphasizing the importance of reason over emotional reactions, Stoicism fosters healthy, harmonious relationships founded on mutual respect and compassion.

Moreover, Stoicism has the potential to inspire individuals to take meaningful social action. When faced with certain challenges or injustices, a stoic individual would be more inclined to engage in problem-solving and active engagement instead of succumbing to anger or hopelessness. This attitude can lead to the development of proactive strategies that address societal problems while maximizing collective well-being.

In contemporary times, Stoicism's concepts of emotional regulation and resilience are increasingly relevant. As modern life progresses at an unprecedented pace, people encounter various stressors that threaten their mental health, relationships, and societal functioning. With its emphasis on cultivating inner strength in the face of adversity, Stoicism offers practical tools for coping with challenges and fostering personal growth that ultimately promotes greater social harmony.

Several organizations today embody the principles of Stoicism in their operating philosophies. For example, Stoic-inspired programs aim at teaching mindfulness techniques to corporate professionals struggling with burnout or providing mental health support to military veterans transitioning back to civilian life. By integrating Stoicism into these settings, practitioners can build resilience, empathy, and healthy coping mechanisms that facilitate a more harmonious work-life balance.

However, critics argue that Stoicism's emphasis on detachment from one's emotions can hinder genuine expression and connection with others. They maintain that emotions can hold valuable information about our needs, desires, and boundaries. While Stoic practices of emotional regulation undoubtedly have merit, it is essential to strike a balance where individuals do not repress their emotions completely but instead learn how to effectively communicate them.

Stoic Ethics and Social Responsibility

Social responsibility has become a crucial aspect of our daily lives. People are increasingly looking for ways to support each other and maintain harmony in society. The age-old philosophy of Stoicism, which focuses on individual growth and self-discipline by seeking wisdom, is highly relevant in this context. Let's analyze Stoic ethics and how they apply to the concept of social responsibility.

A fundamental concept in Stoic philosophy is eudaimonia, or living a virtuous life according to reason. Achieving eudaimonia enables an individual to live harmoniously in society by promoting good values and maintaining order. The four cardinal virtues of Stoicism—wisdom (sophia), courage (andreia), justice (dikaiosyne), and moderation (sophrosyne)—lay the groundwork for the pursuit of eudaimonia.

Wisdom encompasses our ability to discern what is right from wrong, allowing us to make informed decisions that contribute to both personal well-being and the greater good of society. This knowledge helps us navigate various challenges in life while keeping a rational approach to every situation. By developing wisdom, we learn how to deal with diverse values and beliefs in a manner that upholds mutual respect.

Courage goes hand-in-hand with wisdom as it equips us with the mental strength to confront difficult situations or challenges in life without yielding easily to fear or despair. Courage enables us to act on our convictions, even when faced with adversity or criticism from others. In terms of social responsibility, it involves standing up against injustices or defending the rights of the vulnerable.

Justice embodies fairness and unbiased treatment towards all people regardless of their background or circumstances. A crucial aspect of social responsibility involves treating others with respect, acknowledging their needs, and ensuring that everyone has access to resources essential for living a dignified life. By practicing justice, we foster social harmony by upholding all individuals' rights and promoting equal opportunities.

Moderation helps us maintain balance in our lives by avoiding extremes in emotions, thoughts, and actions. Applying moderation to social responsibility means assessing our actions' impact on others and the environment, so as not to cause unnecessary harm. By practicing moderation, we contribute to a sustainable society that preserves resources for the well-being of current and future generations.

Stoic ethics asserts that every individual has innate worth as a rational and social being. This belief underpins our sense of duty towards others, driving us to be socially responsible citizens. We understand that our actions have consequences in the societal fabric, hence the need to act according to reason and virtues.

In line with Stoic thinking, social responsibility is not only a commitment but also an opportunity for self-improvement and growth. By engaging in acts of kindness or advocating for equitable policies, we cultivate virtues within ourselves. Consequently, our actions contribute to attaining eudaimonia for ourselves and those around us.

Furthermore, Stoicism highlights the interconnectedness of the world. The concept of cosmopolitanism, or being a citizen of the universe, emphasizes our responsibility towards all human beings irrespective of geographical boundaries or cultural differences. Stoics believe that we should treat everyone with respect and empathy due to our shared humanity.

Social responsibility goes beyond philanthropy or voluntary work; it extends into the realm of personal conduct, choices, and attitudes. Mindfulness of our decisions' larger implications allows us to participate in building a more empathetic and just society that aligns with Stoic values.

Cosmopolitanism is one prominent concept within Stoic thought that directly relates to social responsibility. The Stoics believed in identifying as citizens of the world, instead of being tied to a specific ethnicity or nationality. They saw every human being as equal and deserving of the same rights, regardless of their origin. This cosmopolitan stance fosters a sense of global responsibility as it pushes us to see the whole planet as our community, transcending national borders and ethnocentric biases.

One way to incorporate Stoic ethics into our understanding of social responsibility is by applying the concept of "preferred indifferent." These are external factors that do not affect one's inner virtues or moral character but can be chosen due to their potential benefits for ourselves and others. For instance, wealth is not inherently good or bad in Stoicism; however, using wealth responsibly for philanthropic purposes aligns with the pursuit of justice.

Another key Stoic teaching related to social responsibility is the distinction between what is within our control and what is not. The Stoics believed that we should focus on those aspects within our sphere of influence while cultivating equanimity towards things beyond our control. To engage in socially responsible activities, we can identify areas where we have the agency to enact positive change – such as volunteering at a local charity or advocating for environmental policies – and accept that some issues may be beyond our direct control.

Advocating for Positive Change

With countless challenges plaguing our modern world, advocating for positive change is not merely a virtue but an indispensable responsibility for each of us. This section will delve deeply into the significance of advocating for positive change within the framework of Stoic philosophy and provide guidance on how to incorporate it into our daily lives.

The roots of Stoic advocacy can be traced back to its founding fathers – Epictetus, Seneca, and Marcus Aurelius – who emphasized the importance of human rationality. But it is not only reason that plays a pivotal role in shaping our character; they believed courage, justice, and wisdom were also essential virtues that every individual must nurture. By cultivating these virtues in concert, we lay the foundation for sustaining positive change.

In advocating for positive change, it's crucial to maintain a Stoic approach: seek improvement from within, embody the virtues you wish to instill in society, and embrace the notion that your sphere of control extends only to your thoughts, emotions, and actions. Effectively driving societal change calls for prudent self-assessment as well as conscious effort.

Hanlon's razor - 'Never attribute to malice what can be adequately explained by ignorance or incompetence' - presents an interesting paradigm from a Stoic perspective. In today's dynamic world, with countless ideas battling for recognition and acceptance, we should give others the benefit of the doubt before assuming their motives are malicious – especially when they are advocating for different forms of positive change.

To embody the concept of advocacy in line with Stoic teachings has several significant dimensions. Here are some key aspects that will guide you in taking on this responsibility:

1. Begin with yourself: To bring about lasting change in society or your environment, you must first establish your personal principles and values. As Marcus Aurelius said, "Look within. Within is the fountain of good, and it will ever bubble up if you will ever dig." By improving yourself, you'll become a robust beacon of resilience, reason, and morality.

2. Practice empathy and understanding: Nurturing the virtues of justice and courage is essential in fostering empathy and understanding with others. Reduce judgment and assumptions; instead, work to develop a conciliatory attitude that transcends divisions and facilitates collaboration for positive change.

3. Lead by example: Exhibit the changes you want to see in the world. Act as an exemplar by prioritizing your well-being, cultivating meaningful relationships, embracing environmental sustainability, or volunteering in your community - the possibilities are limitless. Upholding these changes with conviction demonstrates the effectiveness of your beliefs and encourages others to adopt similar positive behaviors.

4. Influential communication: Harnessing the ability to communicate effectively is instrumental in promoting positive change. Eloquent expressions of ideas can inspire open dialogue, bridge gaps between different factions, and create opportunities for like-minded individuals to join forces in advocating for shared goals.

5. Know your sphere of control: Recognize what you have power over and focus on making the most impact within those bounds. Do not let external factors deter you from carrying out purposeful actions that align with your values.

6. Remain open to new ideas: As an advocate for positive change, it's important to be flexible and adaptive to evolving insights. Be willing to challenge old practices that no longer serve their original purpose or are in opposition to progress – even those that have historically been part of Stoic thought.

7. Remain steadfast during adversity: Lastly, understand that advocating for change is not an easy journey; it's fraught with resistance and setbacks. Embrace these hurdles as opportunities for growth. Encapsulate the resilient nature of Stoics by persevering through obstacles and staying true to your values.

By incorporating these principles into your advocacy efforts, you strengthen your character and help sculpt a better world for generations to come. Remember that every small action contributes to the larger goal of fostering positive change. As Seneca once eloquently expressed, "Let us pick up our books and tracts and learn, and teach, our hands trembling with age; for he who begins too early makes no speed on his journey when he tires."

Part 5: Advanced Stoicism

Part 5 delves deeper into the ethical framework of Stoicism, exploring the enduring values that define a Stoic life. Uncover the essence of true happiness as you journey towards eudaimonia – a flourishing state of being – and absorb yourself in the Stoic code of conduct that guides a purposeful, virtuous existence.

Chapter 10

Stoic Ethics

Stoicism asserts that the highest aim in life is to pursue virtue for its own sake, as virtue is both necessary and sufficient for a life characterized by happiness and tranquility - or "eudaimonia." Stoic ethics focus on becoming a virtuous person; they do so by observing the natural order of the world, understanding our place within it, and using reason to guide our actions accordingly.

The Stoics divide virtue into four categories – wisdom (sophia), courage (andreia), justice (dikaiosyne), and temperance (sophrosyne). Wisdom encompasses the intellectual virtues of knowledge, understanding, and practical wisdom. Courage includes not only physical bravery but also moral courage – standing up for what is right even in difficult situations. Justice involves treating others fairly by giving them what they are due; it fosters harmony within society. Finally, temperance is exercising self-control and moderation in all aspects of life to maintain inner equilibrium.

For the Stoics, developing these virtues requires cultivating a strong moral character. This is achieved through the practice of self-awareness and reflection. By understanding their own emotions, desires, and virtues or vices that manifest within themselves, individuals can work towards strengthening their character.

Several key concepts are essential in advancing one's understanding of Stoic ethics:

1. Dichotomy of Control: The Stoics emphasize that the only things truly within our control are our own judgments, beliefs, desires, and actions. External events and the actions of others are out of our hands; thus, we must learn to focus solely on developing our internal disposition.

2. Amor Fati (Love of Fate): The Stoic ideal is not simply to accept fate but to wholeheartedly embrace whatever comes our way. We ought to perceive life's adversities as opportunities for growth by maintaining a sense of eternal optimism.

3. Logos (Reason or Rationality): While emotions exist within every individual, Stoics seek to maintain rationality as their guiding principle. A mind grounded in reason can manage even the most intense emotions and act accordingly.

4. Oikeiosis (Appropriation or Familiarization): The process of recognizing one's natural affinity with others and the world at large. This is important in fostering empathy and reiterating the interconnectedness of humanity.

5. Negative Visualization: An advanced Stoic practice that involves imagining adverse situations or potential losses to prepare oneself for the harsh realities life may present.

To apply Stoic ethics in modern times, we only need to observe some basic principles:

1. *Focus on what you can control:* When faced with challenges or difficult situations, remember the Dichotomy of Control and devote your energy only towards those aspects where you have influence.
2. *Practice empathy:* In interacting with others, be aware that people inherently possess their struggles and battles. Always treat others kindly and justly.

3. *Seek wisdom from adversity:* Embrace life's hardships as opportunities for growth and learning instead of lamenting about them.
4. *Strive for internal tranquility:* By ensuring a balance between worldly pursuits and inner serenity, we can achieve true peace of mind.

The Stoic Code of Conduct

The foundation of stoic ethics relies on understanding fundamental principles governing human life. These include the nature of existence, orderliness as an inherent quality of reality, and the compatibility between universal laws and individual actions. This section delves into the fundamental principles that shape the Stoic code of conduct.

This Stoic code serves as a practical guide for leading a virtuous life, pursuing inner peace, and attaining tranquility amidst the chaos of the outside world.

1. Understanding the Dichotomy of Control: Central to the Stoic code of conduct is comprehending and accepting the difference between what is within our control and what lies outside it. The only aspects of life that we can truly control are our thoughts, emotions, and actions. External events, other people's opinions or actions are beyond our control.

By recognizing this fundamental distinction, we can avoid emotional turmoil arising from attempting to change or influence situations beyond our reach. Instead, we can focus on refining our internal selves and honing our discipline to tether our happiness to things that we have complete control over.

2. Virtue over Materialism: Stoicism teaches that virtue is the highest good, surpassing material possessions or physical pleasure. A virtuous person embodies traits such as wisdom, courage, justice, and temperance.

The Stoic code directs us to prioritize developing these virtues above accumulating wealth, fame or power. A stoic individual does not attach their self-worth to transient external factors but seeks to cultivate an unwavering moral character.

3. Emotional Mastery through Rational Thinking: Negative emotions such as anger, jealousy or sadness stem from irrational beliefs about reality, which often leads to misplaced judgments. The Stoic code encourages us to use reason to discern these inaccuracies in order to respond rationally to situations.

By questioning whether our beliefs align with reality and discarding those that do not, we can attain emotional stability and prevent distress.

4. Awareness of the Impermanent Nature of Life: The Stoic code encourages us to be mindful of the transient nature of all things, including our own lives. This practice is known as Memento Mori, a reminder of our mortality.

Acknowledging that everything is temporary allows us to appreciate the present moment and not take life for granted. Moreover, this mindset helps in understanding that setbacks, too, shall pass and should not deter us from living virtuous lives.

5. Embracing Adversity: Stoicism acknowledges the inevitability of challenges and adversities in life. Rather than perceiving them as roadblocks or sources of suffering, stoics view difficulties as opportunities to strengthen their inner fortitude.

Developing resilience through adverse experiences refines our character and brings us closer to attaining true happiness rooted in virtue.

6. Remembering that Death is a Part of Life: Death is an integral part of the human experience and not something to be feared or avoided. According to Stoicism, death must be accepted as a natural process and detachment from it will eliminate unnecessary anxieties.

The Stoic code guides us to live each day with purpose, cultivating virtue and practicing wisdom, so that when death arrives, we may face it with equanimity.

7. The Art of Negative Visualization: Negative visualization involves contemplating possible losses or worst-case scenarios without succumbing to fear or anxiety. Instead, it helps us to reinforce gratitude for what we currently have and maintain an appropriate perspective on our desires and attachments.

Used effectively, this practice enables stoics to foster contentment and become more resilient in the face of challenges that life might bring.

8. Practicing Mindfulness: Being present in the moment plays a crucial role in adhering to the Stoic code of conduct. Mindfulness helps us avoid destructive thoughts and emotions by allowing us to focus on our rational responses to any given situation.

By remaining centered in the present, we will not be held hostage by unproductive feelings and can make decisions rooted in reason and virtue.

Living a Stoic Life

It is essential to understand that living a true stoic life goes beyond embracing philosophy. It entails mastering the art of living in accordance with nature and focusing on personal ethics to find inner peace and tranquility. Stoic ethics, being the core aspect of stoic philosophy, is all about rational decision-making, exercising self-control, and understanding ourselves better.

One of the primary teachings in stoic ethics is to contemplate our actions based on their moral significance rather than pursuing pleasure or avoiding pain. Stoics believe that virtues such as courage, wisdom, self-discipline, and justice should be the guiding force behind our decisions. Inner virtue is seen as the ultimate source of happiness and contentment. External circumstances or events have no impact on our well-being if we master these virtues.

To live a stoic life, we must learn to practice self-discipline. Stoic philosophers teach us that discipline leads to freedom. When we govern our impulses, desires, and emotions—instead of letting them control us—we become masters of ourselves. Disciplining ourselves helps us stay focused on our goals and aspirations without succumbing to distractions or further suffering.

Another critical element in stoic ethics is the pursuit of wisdom. True wisdom comes from observing the natural world, examining our own thoughts and behaviors while learning from others' experiences. Wisdom enables us to make more informed decisions when faced with challenges or adversity. To gain wisdom, stoics suggest cultivating a habit of reading books, engaging in meaningful discussions with others who have different perspectives or backgrounds, and self-reflection.

Living a stoic life also involves embracing mental resilience when faced with hardships and setbacks. Instead of allowing adverse events to weaken or discourage us, we must remind ourselves that challenges can serve as opportunities for growth and personal development. The way we respond to setbacks and adversity determines the outcome of any situation. By embracing mental resilience, we can gain wisdom, strength, and learn invaluable lessons from our experiences.

Moreover, living a stoic life means practicing mindfulness in every aspect of our daily lives. By paying attention to our thoughts and actions, we become fully present in each moment, enhancing self-awareness and promoting rational decision-making. Stoic philosophers suggest that mindfulness should be an integral part of our daily routine to help us stay grounded and focused on what truly matters.

Stoics also promote living a life of simplicity. By cherishing simple pleasures and minimizing unnecessary possessions or distractions, we create more room for peace and contentment within our lives. Consuming with intent rather than impulse frees us from the trap of materialism and allows us to focus on innate virtues.

At the heart of stoic ethics is the acceptance of impermanence. Everything in life has a beginning and an end; change is inevitable. Embracing this reality helps us let go of attachments to people or things that may no longer serve us or be within our control. Letting go allows an easier adaptation to change while fostering inner peace.

Additionally, practicing empathy contributes significantly to living a stoic life. Through understanding others' emotions and perspectives despite differences or disagreements, we can foster healthy relationships and avoid conflict stemming from misunderstandings. It is essential to remember that everyone carries their struggles or challenges; being empathetic goes a long way in creating harmony among ourselves and others.

Lastly, living a stoic life means embracing responsibility for every decision made and action taken. Stoic ethics implore us to take ownership of our thoughts, emotions, and actions rather than blame external factors for any unwanted results. Owning up to decisions made gives us the power to learn from our mistakes and grow as individuals.

Let us dive into the essential elements that frame the path towards living a truly stoic life.

1. Virtue as the Highest Good: Within Stoicism, virtue is considered the highest good and is defined as the ultimate value that surpasses all others. Virtue refers to moral excellence, which involves understanding what is truly important in life and acting accordingly.

Virtues can be broadly categorized into four main components: wisdom, courage, justice, and temperance. Wisdom includes knowledge and understanding; courage encompasses endurance and resolution; justice involves fairness and integrity; and temperance embodies moderation and self-control.

These four virtues are interconnected, ensuring that every aspect of one's life – from interpersonal relationships to personal aspirations – is built upon solid ethical foundations.

2. Developing Virtue Through Practice: To embrace advanced stoicism fully, you must strive to develop these virtues actively. Consistent practice improves your capacity for rational thinking and decision-making, making it an integral part of living a stoic life.

Here are some practical steps you can take to grow in virtue:

1. Reflect on your actions: Introspect daily and analyze your thoughts, emotions, and actions to bring awareness to areas that may require improvement.
2. Contemplate on moral examples: Draw inspiration from the lives of virtuous individuals, both historical and contemporary, and emulate their ethical behaviors.
3. Engage in challenging situations: Push yourself out of your comfort zone and find opportunities to demonstrate courage and resilience.

4. Practice forgiveness: Show mercy to both yourself and others, acknowledging that mistakes are a natural part of growth.
5. Live with gratitude: Cultivate a mindset of contentment by recognizing the abundance within your life.

3. Dichotomy of Control: In advanced Stoicism, it is essential to understand the dichotomy of control, which emphasizes that certain aspects of life lie within our control, while others remain outside our influence. This understanding enables us to focus our attention on what we can indeed change or affect – primarily our thoughts, beliefs, actions, and emotions – rather than wasting energy on external circumstances.

Living in accordance with the dichotomy of control helps maintain a consistent practice of Stoic ethics, as we respond thoughtfully and deliberately to life's challenges.

5. Amor Fati-Love Your Fate: The concept of 'Amor Fati,' or love of fate, permeates Stoic ethics. It calls for an acceptance and embrace of all that life brings; be it happiness or sadness, abundance or scarcity. By adopting an attitude of appreciation for every experience and learning from each moment, it becomes possible to develop resilience, resolve, and tranquility in the face of adversity.

Cultivating amor fati in your life demands a persistent practice of reframing events in a positive light while maintaining an open mind for personal growth.

Chapter 11

Stoic Happiness

The Stoic Definition of Happiness

THE STOIC DEFINITION OF HAPPINESS, OR EUDAIMONIA, IS A CENTRAL concept in the philosophy of Stoicism and a core tenet influencing the practical applications of this way of life. Happiness, from the Stoic perspective, is an inner state of tranquility and balance that arises from living consistently with reason and nature. Understanding the Stoic definition of happiness is an important step towards appreciating the wisdom of this ancient philosophy fully and incorporating its insights into everyday life.

Eudaimonia, which translates to "good spirit" or "flourishing," is often equated with happiness in broader philosophical discussions. However, the Stoics saw eudaimonia as a more complex and profound state rooted in different values than conventional definitions typically imply. For them, true happiness was not synonymous with momentary pleasures, superficial successes, or emotional highs but rather with cultivating virtuous character traits and living according to reason in harmony with nature.

Central to the Stoic conception of happiness is their belief in Virtue (arete) as the highest good. Virtue refers to moral excellence – the cultivated disposition to think, feel, and act in ways that are morally right and beneficial. In this sense, Virtue involves developing traits like wisdom, courage, justice, and temperance –attributes that enable individuals to act ethically and achieve a meaningful life. According to Stoicism, by pursuing Virtue as one's primary goal, genuine happiness naturally unfolds.

An essential pillar of the Stoic pursuit of happiness is understanding that certain aspects of life lie beyond our control. External events such as our social status, possessions, or bodily conditions are often not up to us but determined by forces outside our influence. In contrast, our thoughts, judgments, and actions - which ultimately give rise to our experience - are within our dominion. The freedom granted by recognizing this distinction empowers individuals to focus on personal growth and contribute positively to the world around them.

In the quest for happiness, the Stoic philosopher Epictetus advised adherents to distinguish between what lies in their power and what does not. By accepting what cannot be changed, and conscientiously working towards optimizing one's mental attitudes and behaviors, individuals can remain resilient in the face of adversity. This detachment from externals is essential for maintaining equanimity or an untroubled mind – a vital aspect of happiness according to the Stoics.

Serenity, or apatheia, is another significant dimension of happiness in Stoic thought. It refers to a calmness of spirit that arises from the knowledge that an individual is acting virtuously and free from irrational desires. Apathetic individuals are not cold or indifferent but rather possess an inner equilibrium that allows them to experience joy, avoid destructive emotions like anger or envy, and engage with life fully without becoming ruled by its vicissitudes.

This stoic concept of happiness is closely related to another foundational doctrine in Stoicism – amor fati, or "love of fate." To love fate is to embrace whatever path unfolds with openness and determination, allowing oneself to grow through embracing challenges, setbacks, and even suffering. In doing so, one cultivates the resilience needed to navigate life's unpredictable nature effectively while working towards creating meaning amidst uncertainty.

The pursuit of happiness in Stoicism emphasizes an ongoing journey towards self-improvement rather than a fixed end-state. It begins with introspection – reflecting on one's values, beliefs, and behaviors – followed by identifying areas for growth and committing to cultivating virtue progressively. This process requires humility and patience as individuals confront their weaknesses, but it is through this effort that genuine contentment becomes accessible.

One practical technique that can help in cultivating Stoic happiness is meditation on adversity (premeditatio malorum). By envisioning potential problems that may arise in life and preparing oneself to face them with tempered expectations, it becomes possible to develop resilience and avoid being overwhelmed when challenges inevitably arise. Furthermore, this practice increases gratitude for the present moment, fostering a sense of contentment as one appreciates the gifts of their current circumstances without craving more.

Pursuing Eudaimonia

In order to understand why eudaimonia emerged as such a critical notion in Stoicism, it is first necessary to review the philosophy's essential tenets. For the Stoics, life's ultimate purpose is not found in material wealth or sensual pleasure but resides, instead, in attaining a form of harmony with oneself and with nature. This harmony is accomplished through several key principles: accepting what one cannot control, cultivating virtue through wisdom and moral strength, exercising reason in decision-making, and actualizing an authentic sense of inner tranquility. It is within these guiding principles that the pursuit of eudaimonia unfolds.

The first step in pursuing eudaimonia through Stoicism involves developing a sense of acceptance toward our finite control over external events. As Epictetus wisely declared, "Happiness and freedom begin with a clear understanding of one principle: some things are within our control, and some things are not." By recognizing the limitations of our agency in worldly matters and relinquishing any anxiety or desire for outcomes beyond our influence, we enable ourselves to cultivate resilience and adaptability in the face of adversity. This approach ultimately leads us closer to eudaimonia since we are no longer held captive by external happenstance or volatile emotions but can engage confidently with whatever life brings forth.

Next, embracing virtue as a primary aim for living prepares us for eudaimonic flourishing. Virtue – honesty, courage, justice, and prudence – aligns us with moral integrity and infuses our actions with a sense of purpose and authenticity. In cultivating these qualities, we derive genuine and sustained satisfaction that transcends temporary pleasures or fleeting distractions. As Seneca eloquently stated, "A gem cannot be polished without friction, nor a man perfected without trials." The Stoic view sees an intrinsic link between the pursuit of virtue and the enduring realization of eudaimonia.

Crucial to our pursuit of eudaimonia is also the employment of reason in decision-making. In Stoicism, the rational mind is highly revered; it is considered the cornerstone upon which our perceptions are formed and judgments are made. Deploying reasoned thought processes helps us maintain perspective, make informed choices, and avoid impulsive behavior propelled by misguided emotions. Marcus Aurelius affirmed this conviction in his Meditations: "Everything we hear is an opinion, not a fact. Everything we see is a perspective, not the truth." By diligently applying reason to life's circumstances, we nurture insight and wisdom that propel us toward eudaimonia.

Lastly, as attaining inner tranquility remains central to the Stoic philosophy, achieving eudaimonia necessitates cultivating equanimity amidst external turbulence. This inner calm stems from our ability to remain unperturbed in the face of adversity while maintaining composure despite external turmoil or emotional provocation. As Epictetus advised, "Do not seek to have events happen as you want them to but instead want them to happen as they do happen, and your life will go smoothly." Embracing this disposition allows us to navigate chaos with grace and emerge from the trials unscathed – thus embodying eudaimonic flourishing.

Acquiring this state of well-being mandates consistent practice and dedication as we strive to align our thoughts and actions with Stoic principles. Furthermore, pursuing eudaimonia requires us to engage in continuous self-reflection and personal introspection, ensuring that we remain dedicated to the Stoic path even when confronted with life's inevitable challenges.

Part 6: Mastering Stoicism

As you continue your odyssey into the heart of Stoicism, Part 6 tackles the obstacles and challenges that may hinder your progress. Find out how to establish a rewarding, sustainable Stoic routine amidst criticism, and garner practical tips for living each day abundantly as a devoted follower of this ancient yet timeless philosophy.

Chapter 12

Stoic Challenges and Obstacles

Despite its many benefits, practicing stoicism can also present various challenges and obstacles that need overcoming. Below are some of the most common hurdles faced by those embracing the Stoic way of life, offering practical guidance to navigate these tests successfully.

1. Initial Resistance to Change: Embracing stoicism often necessitates significant alterations in one's attitudes and behaviors to align with the teachings of this philosophical school. These changes may be met with internal resistance as individuals are naturally inclined to maintain their pre-existing perspectives and habits.

Overcoming this hurdle requires individuals to identify and evaluate the limiting beliefs that contribute to such resistance. For instance, one might be prone to irrational thinking patterns or have a skewed perception of control over external circumstances. Recognizing these impediments provides an opportunity for honest self-assessment, reframing negative thought patterns towards a more rational outlook, enabling progress on the path of stoicism.

2. Difficulty Implementing Stoic Practices: One notable difficulty faced when embracing stoicism is consistently applying its core teachings in everyday life. The demands of modern living can create situations in which it is challenging to practice emotional detachment or remember that happiness comes from within.

In response to this obstacle, stoic practitioners should develop daily rituals and cues reminding themselves of the principles they wish to internalize. Establishing routines such as journaling or meditation can facilitate introspection and focus on implementing stoic values daily.

Additionally, individuals might benefit from seeking support networks consisting of fellow practitioners providing mutual encouragement in facing challenges typical to a Stoic lifestyle.

3. Struggling with Emotions: A fundamental trait of stoicism is the cultivation of emotional resilience that allows one to remain calm and collected under varying circumstances. However, achieving mastery over one's emotions can prove elusive as emotional reactions are deeply ingrained human responses.

One key to overcoming this obstacle lies in accepting emotions without judgment and recognizing them as natural occurrences. Stoic practitioners need to remember that experiencing emotions is not inherently counterproductive; rather, the issue lies in irrational emotional responses overwhelming reason. By observing emotions without succumbing to them, individuals can create space for rational thought, maintaining equilibrium and reasoned decision-making.

4. Misunderstanding Stoicism: Misconceptions about stoicism can potentially derail one's progress in fully integrating its teachings into their life. A common misunderstanding is that stoicism advocates for emotional suppression or a lack of empathy. Such viewpoints can lead to resistance among those who perceive stoicism as lacking compassion or connection.

Clarifying and deepening one's understanding of this philosophical system is crucial to mitigate these misconceptions. Stoicism encourages emotional responsibility, owning one's emotions, and learning to act from reason rather than being driven by uncontrolled emotional responses.

5. Temptations of Modern Society: The distractions and temptations present in contemporary society can hinder the adoption of a stoic lifestyle. The external noise of constant connectivity or the emphasis on material success might cause deviations from Stoic values centered around inner tranquility and self-mastery.

To preserve their commitment to stoicism, individuals should establish boundaries that guard against distractions threatening their focus on personal growth and development. Periodically disengaging from material concerns by practicing voluntary discomfort can also foster a sense of gratitude and resilience, strengthening one's adherence to stoic principles amid societal pressures.

6. Maintaining Consistency and Motivation: Maintaining unwavering motivation to practice stoicism is undoubtedly challenging, especially in the face of setbacks or disappointments.

To cultivate perseverance through trials, individuals must foster an intrinsic drive by identifying their personal motivations for adopting this lifestyle. Additionally, breaking down long-term goals into smaller, incremental objectives may contribute to sustained enthusiasm and progress over time.

Overcoming Common Hurdles

As we navigate through life, we are bound to face numerous hurdles that may impede our progress and hinder our personal growth. The practice of Stoicism offers us invaluable tools to overcome these obstacles and elevate our mindset. Let's explore common challenges people face and examine how Stoic principles can help us triumph over them.

1. Fear of Failure: Fear of failure is a powerful deterrent that often holds us back from taking risks or pursuing ambitious goals. According to the Stoics, fear itself is not the issue; rather, it's our perception of fear that becomes the problem. Epictetus said, "It's not what happens to you but how you react to it that matters."

To overcome the fear of failure, we should remind ourselves that stagnation from inaction also leads to failure. By embracing potential setbacks as learning experiences, we can alter our perception and adopt a growth mindset. With such an outlook, we turn each failure into an opportunity for personal development and strengthening our resilience.

2. Social Anxieties and Negative Relationships: In a world where social media often dictates self-worth, building meaningful connections can be challenging. The Stoic practice emphasizes focusing on what lies within our control – our thoughts, beliefs, and actions.

To navigate social anxieties and foster healthier relationships, we must first cultivate self-awareness and recognize how external influences impact our well-being. Practicing Stoic principles like empathy, understanding, and open communication can transform negative relationships by empowering us to prioritize personal values over societal pressures.

3. Procrastination: Procrastination is a deep-rooted habit that hinders productivity and leaves us feeling overwhelmed as deadlines approach. Seneca said, "We suffer more often in imagination than reality," highlighting how procrastination is often fueled by imagined fears or obstacles rather than genuine ones.

Combat procrastination by breaking tasks into smaller, manageable steps and focusing on completing each step one at a time. Stoicism teaches us to live in the present moment—by concentrating on the task at hand and not the enormity of the larger project, we can gradually chip away at our workload and reduce the burden of procrastination.

4. Inadequate Work-Life Balance: Striking an optimal balance between our personal lives and careers can be challenging, especially when striving for success in both domains. However, neglecting either responsibility can lead to burnout and adverse effects on mental health. According to Marcus Aurelius, "The happiness of your life depends upon the quality of your thoughts."

To establish a healthy work-life balance, practice mindfulness and self-reflection, allowing yourself space for emotional growth and rejuvenation. Ensure that you allocate time each day for self-care activities, family, hobbies or relaxation alongside your professional pursuits. Stoicism reminds us that external success is meaningless if it comes at the expense of inner tranquility.

5. Indecision: Constantly second-guessing ourselves can leave us paralyzed by indecision. As the Stoics have taught us, clarity of thought and a strong sense of personal values are crucial in making sound decisions.

Practice introspection to recognize your core beliefs and consider whether potential choices are aligned with those values. Engage in practical wisdom and differentiate between what lies within your control and what does not. Accepting that we have limited control over certain outcomes can liberate us from indecision by focusing our attention on factors we can genuinely influence.

Dealing with Stoic Criticism

Stoicism approach offers tools to help us contend with hardships, develop practical wisdom, and attain inner peace. However, it is also essential to acknowledge and confront the various criticisms that it has faced throughout its existence.

Let's address some of the most prevalent critiques of Stoicism and provide you with techniques to incorporate these insights into your practice. By addressing these critiques head-on, we hope to help you build a more nuanced understanding of Stoicism. As Seneca once observed, "Difficulties strengthen the mind as labor does the body."

1. Lack of Emotional Expression: One significant critique against Stoicism pivots around the suppression or avoidance of emotion. Critics argue that this aspect can lead to emotional detachment and hinder interpersonal relationships. To address this issue, instead of completely suppressing our emotions, we should try acknowledging, understanding, and managing them.

Stoics strive for rationality, but it does not mean they are devoid of feelings. Rather, their focus lies in differentiating between what they can control (their thoughts) and what they cannot control (external events). By recognizing our emotions without being overwhelmed by them, we can maintain a balanced perspective and act more objectively in frustrating situations.

2. Navigating Apathy: Since Stoicism teaches us to accept inevitable outcomes with equanimity, there is sometimes a risk of becoming apathetic – becoming indifferent to necessary change or action. However, genuine Stoic philosophy does not advocate for passivity; rather it encourages informed action when appropriate. To avoid slipping into apathy while practicing Stoicism:

1. *Cultivate gratitude:* Reflect daily on the simple joys of life while simultaneously reminding yourself of the fleeting nature of things. Gratitude can help you appreciate life's value and motivate you to act when needed.
2. *Embrace responsibility:* Acknowledge obligations toward yourself and others. Take your duties seriously, while remembering the importance of prosoche (paying attention) and how your actions impact others.

3. The Absolutism of Virtue: Critics often point out that Stoicism's focus on virtue can lead to an all-or-nothing attitude that overlooks the complexities of human experiences. To ensure that we do not fall into this trap, it is crucial to practice humility and acknowledge our consistent evolution.

View yourself as a "work-in-progress" and recognize that attaining perfect wisdom or virtue is not a feasible goal. Instead, strive to learn from each experience, both good and bad, on a journey of constant self-improvement.

4. Overemphasis on Self-Reliance: Stoicism emphasizes the importance of self-sufficiency – reducing our reliance on material possessions, other people's opinions, or external circumstances for happiness. Critics argue that this might make Stoics appear egocentric or incapable of seeking help when needed.

Address this criticism by continuously reflecting on the interdependence present in life:

1. *Support networks:* Recognize the value in fostering meaningful relationships with family and friends.
2. *Cooperation:* Actively participate in your community, contributing to others' well-being by extending assistance when it is within your power.

5. Failure to Acknowledge Circumstantial Inequality: Stoicism's principles apply universally – regardless of an individual's social background or personal situation. Critics claim that this may lead to an insensitivity towards certain issues and injustices.

In response to this criticism, remember that while you cannot control what happens in society at large, you can act justly within your sphere of influence:

- Be compassionate with ourselves and others during difficult circumstances.
- Speak up and act against injustice when it is within your control. However, do not become consumed with frustration if challenges persist – this is where the principles of Stoicism can aid in maintaining equanimity.

Chapter 13

The Stoic Lifestyle

Practical Tips for Embracing Stoicism Daily

Stoicism in the modern world may seem like a complex and challenging philosophy to follow, but by breaking it down into practical tips and integrating them into your daily life, you can begin to approach life with a calm, rational demeanor that is more resilient to external stressors. Below are various methods for embracing Stoicism daily.

1. Practice Mindfulness: Mindfulness is the foundation of Stoicism. It involves paying attention to your thoughts and actions without judgment. Start by setting aside a few minutes each day to focus on your breathing and observe your thoughts without judgment or attachment. As you develop this habit, extend your practice to include other activities such as washing dishes or walking.

2. Cultivate Gratitude: Gratitude can dramatically change how we perceive and interact with the world around us. Each day, take a moment to reflect on three things that you are grateful for. It could be something basic such as having food on the table, relationships with loved ones, or a recent achievement. This practice will help you develop an appreciation for what you already have and reduce the desire for more.

3. Differentiate Between What Is Within Your Control and What Is Not: Recognizing what is within our control and what is not allows us to focus our energy on aspects of our lives where we can make a difference. Every day, remind yourself that there are certain things beyond your control – like the weather, others' thoughts and actions, or global events – that you cannot change.

4. Journal Your Thoughts: Journaling can be an effective way of releasing emotions and getting your thoughts down on paper. It enables us to gain perspective on situations and can be an invaluable tool in developing self-awareness. Set some time aside each day to write about your emotions, accomplishments, challenges you've faced, or lessons learned from applying Stoic principles in your daily life.

5. Reflect on the Stoic Virtues: Stoicism revolves around four fundamental virtues: wisdom, courage, justice, and temperance. Each day, reflect on how you can practice these virtues in your life. Consider how you can cultivate wisdom through learning and experience, display courage in facing adversity, act justly in your dealings with others, and exercise temperance with self-control and moderation.

6. Embrace Discomfort: Challenging yourself to embrace discomfort helps build mental resilience and allows you to understand that external circumstances do not define your happiness. Try taking cold showers, fasting occasionally, or engaging in physical activities that push you out of your comfort zone. Not only will this strengthen your resolve, but it will also prepare you for any hardships that may come your way.

7. Practice Negative Visualization: Negative visualization involves imagining possible negative outcomes or things going wrong to help prepare for adversity and cope with potential disappointment. Spend a few minutes each day contemplating the loss of something you value (such as a job or a relationship) so that if it does happen, you are prepared to deal with it rationally instead of being emotionally distraught.

8. Meditate on Death: Stoics frequently remind themselves of life's fragility and the inevitability of death. By doing so, they develop a sense of urgency to make the most out of the present moment and fully appreciate their experiences without taking anything for granted. Spend a few moments reflecting on these ideas to help put life's daily challenges into perspective.

9. Exercise Empathy: Empathy fosters understanding and compassion toward others who may be experiencing adversity or behaving unreasonably due to their own internal struggles. When encountering someone difficult or challenging situations, make an effort to see things from their perspective and withhold judgment. This can lead to more harmonious relationships and improved conflict resolution.

10. Develop a Stoic Routine: Integrating Stoic principles into your daily routine will help build consistency in your practice and solidify these habits in your life. Your routine may include morning or evening reflections, daily journaling, mindfulness exercises, studying Stoic texts, or engaging in acts of kindness.

Creating Your Stoic Routine

As you progress in your journey to embody these ideals, it is essential to develop a Stoic routine that brings structure to your everyday life. The purpose of this routine is to create habits that align with the central tenets of Stoicism, promoting rationality, mindfulness, and emotional mastery. Let's examine various techniques to integrate Stoic mindfulness practices into your daily life, ultimately crafting a personalized routine that works best for you.

1. Morning Meditation: As Marcus Aurelius said, "A man's life is dyed by the color of his thoughts." To begin each day enveloped in the spirit of Stoicism, one should engage in morning meditation. This practice entails pausing before starting your day's tasks and taking some time to review your guiding principles or works by famous Stoics like Marcus Aurelius, Epictetus, or Seneca.

During morning meditation, focus on internal reflection and evaluate areas where you have made progress towards embracing Stoic virtues, as well as those where improvement is needed. As you review these works and reflect on their teachings, contemplate how they can be applied to situations you may encounter throughout the day.

2. Journaling: Journaling is an essential aspect of creating your Stoic routine. Daily journaling allows you to track your progress along the path of Stoicism and serves as an outlet for self-examination and reflection. Make it a habit to record moments where you successfully applied the teachings of Stoicism and instances where you fell short. By consistently journaling about your experiences and emotions, you can develop a deeper understanding of yourself and better identify areas that require improvement.

3. Objective Evaluation: Stoicism teaches us that our negative emotions are often rooted in irrational beliefs. Through objective evaluation, we can assess our emotional states calmly and without judgment while considering the events that triggered these emotions. During this practice, step back and objectively assess the situation, seeking to understand it from a rational perspective free from any misinterpretations.

By evaluating your emotional reactions and the situations that trigger them in an unbiased manner, you can gain control over your emotions and achieve greater harmony with your Stoic values.

4. Control Over Your Perception: One of Stoicism's central teachings is recognizing the distinction between what we can and cannot control. It becomes crucial, then, to develop an ability to pause and evaluate whether the distressing circumstances we face are within our power to change or something we must accept.

Incorporating this practice into your routine allows you to evaluate daily challenges in alignment with Stoic principles. By reflecting on the actual source of distress – whether internal or external – you can develop inner tranquility and improve your decision-making process.

5. Nighttime Reflection: As night falls and you begin to unwind from the day's demands, take a moment to engage in nighttime reflection. Review your actions throughout the day, evaluating if they align with your Stoic values and identifying any progress made or areas that need improvement.

During this evening practice, consider any obstacles you encountered during the day and seek to apply Stoic teachings in overcoming such difficulties. It is also an opportunity to express gratitude for the lessons provided by these challenges and contemplate how these experiences have contributed to deepening your understanding of Stoic values.

Part 7: The Future Of Stoicism

The final part of "Stoicism Bible" envisions a future where Stoicism thrives within modern culture and institutions. Assess the role of Stoicism in our technology-driven era, alongside its impact on digital mindfulness practices. Inspire future generations by integrating elements of Stoic teachings into education, equipping young minds with resilience and wisdom to face life's inevitable hurdles.

Chapter 14

Stoicism in the Digital Age

Applying Stoicism in a Technology-Driven World

In today's technology-driven world, our everyday lives are filled with countless distractions and stressors. From social media to emails, the constant flow of information can make it difficult to focus on the present moment and maintain inner peace. Applying stoic principles to our interactions with technology can provide us with a valuable roadmap to navigate these challenges and bring balance into our lives.

Wisdom involves understanding how to act in accordance with reason and discerning the difference between what is within our control and what is not. In a technology-driven world, applying wisdom means recognizing that while we can't control everything that appears on our devices, we can control how we interact with them.

A simple exercise in applying wisdom to technology usage is to designate specific times throughout the day when you check your phone or device, such as only checking your email during work hours or setting aside time for social media browsing. By being methodical about when you engage with technology, you'll regain control over your attention.

When it comes to justice, practicing fairness and kindness towards others is critical. With technology blurring the lines between public and private matters, seeking justice involves respecting other people's boundaries and considering how your digital actions impact them. One example is being cautious when sharing someone else's information or images online without permission. Additionally, engaging in constructive conversations rather than online trolling promotes respectful discourse.

Developing courage is an essential stoic virtue for facing modern challenges brought by technology. Confronting uncomfortable truths or admitting mistakes on social media platforms requires courage. This can be done by owning up to your errors and acknowledging differing opinions without resorting to hostility. By embracing vulnerability, we can foster positive growth and set an example for others to follow.

Temperance is the practice of self-restraint and moderation in our actions. When applied to technology, it means being mindful of the amount of time spent on devices, striving for balance in our digital and real-world interactions. To practice temperance with technology, consider implementing a digital detox or taking periodic breaks throughout the day from screens.

Moreover, the stoic concept of focusing only on what is within our control can be a powerful tool for managing stress in the digital age. Numerous external factors are beyond our control, such as global events or the opinions of others. To avoid being overwhelmed by news alerts or the bombardment of information on social media, concentrate on only those aspects that are within your power to affect.

Mindfulness is another key aspect of stoicism that offers great benefits in our technology-driven world. We can practice mindfulness when using technology by being aware of how it affects our thoughts and emotions. For instance, before mindlessly scrolling through social media feeds, pause and assess how you feel. If you notice that certain content evokes negative feelings or that your screen time is detracting from more meaningful experiences, make adjustments accordingly.

Lastly, it's vital to cultivate gratitude as part of the stoic practice in our modern lives. Amidst the constant noise and distractions presented by technology, we can easily lose sight of the positive aspects in our lives.

Taking a moment each day to reflect on what we're thankful for – such as personal achievements, relationships, or beautiful sunsets – can help establish a mindset focused on appreciation rather than discontent.

Stoic Mindfulness in the Digital Era

Before delving into how we can foster Stoic mindfulness in today's hyperconnected world, it's essential to understand what it entails. The essence of Stoicism lies in recognizing that while we cannot control external circumstances, we can control our interpretations and reactions to them. Therefore, Stoic mindfulness means cultivating a peaceful state of mind by applying rational thinking to manage our thoughts and emotions.

Incorporating Stoicism into daily life amid the digital era may seem challenging. However, its principles align well with modern psychology, making them relevant today.

Here are some practical ways to practice Stoic mindfulness in our fast-paced digital age:

1. Limit your exposure to digital stimuli: Inundation with content from social media platforms, emails, messages, and videos can overwhelm our minds, adversely affecting our mental health. To protect ourselves from this sensory overload, it is essential to establish boundaries on our device usage.

Try allocating specific times during the day for checking email or social media accounts, turning off notifications for non-urgent matters, or using digital tools like website blockers or app limits to help maintain focus on essential tasks.

2. Practice self-awareness: As the bedrock of Stoicism, self-awareness enables us to recognize our emotions and thoughts objectively. In a digital world dotted with stimuli vying for our attention, developing a deeper sense of self-awareness is essential for mental stability.

Try mindfulness meditation techniques, such as deep breathing exercises or body scans, to grow more attuned to your thoughts and emotions. Throughout the day, take pauses to self-reflect. Ask yourself how your digital consumption is shaping your feelings and whether it aligns with your values.

3. Accept the impermanence of life: The rapid acceleration of technology might exacerbate anxieties about failure or unmet expectations. Stoicism encourages acknowledging that life is transient, prompting us to live in the present moment rather than fixating on an uncertain future.

To develop this mindset, reflect on previous challenges or failures and recognize how they shaped your life positively. Remind yourself that you have weathered past storms and remember that challenges are an inevitable part of life's ever-changing nature.

4. Employ negative visualization: While it may appear counterintuitive, contemplating potential hurdles or setbacks can actually promote gratitude and resilience. By visualizing unfavorable outcomes, you prepare yourself mentally for adversity while also appreciating your current circumstances.

Take a few moments in your day to envision plausible obstacles you might face—be it work-related or personal challenges—and consider potential ways of overcoming them. This approach will help reduce anxiety when facing real problems and promote a more balanced emotional state.

5. Cultivate virtuous habits: In our digitally permeated environment, it can be easy to fall prey to unproductive habits or vices like procrastination and addiction to social media. Stoicism emphasizes the crucial role of virtues in living a contented life.

Identify areas where you can nurture virtuous habits—such as fortitude in dealing with setbacks or discipline in sticking to routines—and consciously integrate them into your daily activities. Over time, these habits will establish themselves as a cornerstone of your character, enabling you to deal with emotional turmoil and external events calmly.

Chapter 15

Inspiring Future Generations

Teaching Stoicism to the Next Generation

AMIDST POLITICAL, ECONOMIC, AND ENVIRONMENTAL INSTABILITY, young people are tasked with navigating an increasingly complex landscape. It has never been more important for them to have a foundation of wisdom, resilience, and a strong moral compass to guide them. As we endeavor to impart these invaluable lessons to future generations, one ancient philosophy stands out as particularly relevant and timeless: Stoicism.

Stoicism is a philosophy that originated in Greece over two thousand years ago. Its core tenets emphasize the need for individuals to find inner peace by practicing self-discipline, focusing on what is within their control, and accepting life's inevitable adversities with strength and grace. Below are practical ways in which we can teach Stoicism to the next generation and equip them with the tools they need to lead fulfilling lives.

1. Start Early: Introducing Stoic concepts at a young age can help lay a strong foundation for children's emotional and mental well-being. One way to do this is through storytelling that incorporates core Stoic beliefs such as embracing challenges instead of running away from them or practicing gratitude despite life's hiccups. By consistently integrating these ideas into discussions and reading materials, you can gradually instill Stoic values in children's minds.

2. Model Stoic Behavior: One of the most effective ways to teach Stoicism is by modeling it yourself. Show children how you focus on what you can control rather than fretting about what lies beyond your grasp. When faced with setbacks, demonstrate how patience, resilience, and determination can help overcome obstacles. Discuss your actions openly with children so they can understand your thought process and see Stoicism in action.

3. Engage in Purposeful Dialogues: The importance of engaging in open dialogue with children about moral principles cannot be overstated. Explain why resilience and emotional control are vital attributes and how adopting a Stoic mindset can help them develop these qualities. Encourage them to think critically about life and discuss real-world examples that illustrate Stoicism in practice. In doing so, you will be fostering their ability to analyze situations objectively and to develop their own moral compass.

4. Engage with Stoic Literature: Reading the works of prominent Stoic philosophers like Seneca, Epictetus, and Marcus Aurelius can give children a profound understanding of this philosophical tradition. Provide age-appropriate translations of these texts to make them more accessible to younger readers, or find modern adaptations that depict Stoic principles in relatable terms.

5. Reflect on Emotions: Teach children the importance of reflecting on their emotions and understanding the underlying causes behind them. By cultivating self-awareness, they will be better able to regulate their emotions in difficult situations. This is a key aspect of Stoicism that promotes inner peace and resilience.

6. Practice Gratitude: Cultivating gratitude is a powerful way to help children appreciate the value of life's simpler aspects. Encourage them to express appreciation for what they have daily, or maintain a gratitude journal where they can record moments that remind them of life's blessings.

7. Engage in Community Service: Volunteer work can help children develop empathy and humility while teaching them about social responsibility. It also exposes them to real-life instances where they can apply Stoic principles such as prioritizing the welfare of others over personal interests or finding inner peace amidst adversity.

8. Encourage Meditation: Meditation is an essential component of Stoicism that leads to increased self-awareness and emotional regulation. Introduce children to simple meditation exercises that they can practice independently or as part of a guided routine at home or in school.

10. Teach By Example: Finally, be an example of a good role model by demonstrating your commitment to living according to Stoic principles. Embody the virtues of courage, wisdom, justice, and temperance in your daily life, and children will be inspired to emulate you.

Stoicism in Education

Introducing the principles of Stoicism within educational systems could prove immensely beneficial not only for students themselves but also for society as a whole. At the core of Stoicism lies a fundamental understanding that personal well-being and happiness largely hinge on the way we think, perceive, and react to the world around us. For educators to inspire future generations with this philosophy, it's all about creating an environment where these values are promoted through lessons, demonstrations, and practical application.

Let's discuss how Stoicism can be applied to the educational system in order to more effectively prepare students for the challenges they may face beyond the classroom. We'll touch on its relevance in fostering resilience, critical thinking, emotional intelligence, and ethical values.

1. Enhancing Resilience: One crucial trait that is increasingly recognized as critical in today's fast-paced world is resilience. Given that change is constant and adversity inevitable, instilling within students a strong foundation of resilience through stoic teachings can be instrumental in helping them navigate life's challenges.

Educators can imbue resilience in their classrooms by adopting a few key strategies. First, they should foster a growth mindset — the idea that skills and abilities can improve through hard work and perseverance. By encouraging students to adopt this approach, they are essentially arming them with the confidence and adaptability required to overcome adversity.

Secondly, teachers should actively promote self-awareness among students. They can organize exercises or discussions that encourage reflection on personal strengths, weaknesses, values, and goals. In doing so, learners develop a stronger sense of self — enabling them to better understand their emotions, reactions, and responses when faced with difficult situations.

2. Cultivating Critical Thinking: Another indispensable skill for future generations is critical thinking. The ability to think analytically, evaluate evidence, and make reasoned decisions is essential in a world that's becoming increasingly complex. Thankfully, Stoicism—with its focus on rationality—is custom-built to develop this very skill.

As educators teach the tenets of Stoicism, they will invariably foster in their students a strong sense of self-awareness and logical reasoning needed to think critically. By exploring the works of great stoic philosophers such as Epictetus and Seneca, students learn that objectivity, reflection, and logical analysis are central components of effective problem-solving.

3. Developing Emotional Intelligence: With mental health emerging as an increasingly significant global concern, the need for individuals to possess high levels of emotional intelligence has grown dramatically. Stoic teachings are uniquely positioned to fill this void by helping students understand and regulate their emotions.

When educators infuse the principles of Stoicism into their curriculum, they empower students to recognize the role emotions play in decision-making. By prompting students to regularly practice self-reflection and consider the long-term consequences of their actions, educators strengthen their ability to healthily process emotions—an essential component of emotional intelligence.

4. Encouraging Ethical Values: In order for future generations to excel in increasingly global and connected societies, it's vital that they demonstrate unwavering ethical values. Unsurprisingly, this is yet another area in which Stoic teachings excel.

By studying the stoic principles such as courage, wisdom, justice, and temperance, students are encouraged to reflect on how these virtues apply in their daily lives. This self-reflection fosters moral growth and increases appreciation for living an honorable life.

Conclusion: The Everlasting Wisdom of Stoicism

For over two thousand years, Stoicism has inspired countless individuals across the globe to seek tranquility, focus on rational decision-making, and accept reality while responding constructively. One of the most significant aspects of Stoic philosophy is its emphasis on practicing virtues such as self-discipline, resilience, and humility. These virtues empower individuals to maintain a balanced life while confronting everyday challenges with rationality instead of letting emotions override their judgment. This foundation allows us to approach complex situations with clarity and pragmatism.

The teachings of Epictetus, Seneca, and Marcus Aurelius encourage our detachment from material possessions, emphasizing the transitory nature of life and that real contentment can only radiate from within. Recognizing that external factors are mainly out of our control is a cornerstone of Stoic thought, leading us to focus on our internal development and character growth. Consequently, Stoic principles cultivate inner strength to face adversity with courage and confidence.

Furthermore, the wisdom in practicing mindfulness in our daily routines fosters gratitude for the present moment and provides a keener insight into our purpose in life. The Stoic belief in premeditation malorum –

contemplating potential adversities – prepares us mentally to weather difficult times by developing strategies to overcome them.

Stoicism's enduring relevance in today's world highlights its adaptability across cultures and changing social norms. Many individuals turn towards Stoicism when searching for solace amid frantic lives or finding a way to remain centered amidst chaos. The philosophy imparts invaluable lessons fostering resilience, well-being, self-awareness, and unwavering rationality.

Utilizing the everlasting wisdom of Stoicism will undoubtedly contribute positively towards personal growth. Embracing the core tenets of this insightful philosophy equips us to navigate life's challenges tactfully while fostering virtues leading to a more balanced, harmonious, and fulfilling existence.

As the Stoic philosopher Seneca once stated, "It is not the man who has too little that is poor, but the one who hankers after more." By internalizing this powerful insight, we can better focus on what truly matters in life: finding inner peace, developing our character, and living in harmony with ourselves and the world. Let the legacy of Stoicism continue to inspire us and guide our endeavors for generations to come.

Made in the USA
Middletown, DE
11 November 2023